To our children: Austin, Keaton, and Whitney.

And to our son-in-law, Daniel, and our future in-laws and grandchildren.

May we continue to grow together!

HOW TO TALK WITH YOUR KIDS ABOUT SEX

RODNEY & TRACI WRIGHT

HOW TO TALK WITH YOUR KIDS ABOUT SEX

© Copyright Pure Desire Ministries International
Printed in the United States of America
ALL RIGHTS RESERVED
www.puredesire.org

Published by
Pure Desire Ministries International
www.puredesire.org | Troutdale, Oregon | November 2019

ISBN 978-1-943291-13-7

No part of this publication may be reproduced, stored in a retrieval system, or transmitted in any form by any means—electronic, mechanical, photocopying, recording or otherwise—without prior written consent of Pure Desire Ministries International, except as provided by the United States of America copyright law.

Unless otherwise noted, all Scripture quotations are from THE HOLY BIBLE, NEW INTERNATIONAL VERSION®, NIV®. Copyright © 1973, 1978, 1984, 2011 by Biblica, Inc.®. Used by permission. All rights reserved worldwide.

Scripture quotations noted NASB are from the NEW AMERICAN STANDARD BIBLE®. Copyright © 1960, 1962, 1963, 1968, 1971, 1972, 1973, 1975, 1977, 1995 by The Lockman Foundation. Used by permission.

Scripture quotations noted MSG are from The Message. Copyright © 1993, 1994, 1995, 1996, 2000, 2001, 2002. Used by permission of NavPress Publishing Group.

Scripture quotations noted NLT are from the Holy Bible, New Living Translation. Copyright © 1996, 2004, 2015 by Tyndale House Foundation. Used by permission of Tyndale House Publishers, Inc., Carol Stream, Illinois 60188. All rights reserved.

Scripture quotations noted NRSVA are from the New Revised Standard Version Bible: Anglicised Edition, copyright © 1989, 1995 the Division of Christian Education of the National Council of the Churches of Christ in the United States of America. Used by permission. All rights reserved.

Content editing by Heather Kolb

Cover design, interior design, and typesetting by Elisabeth Pearce

CONTENTS

PREFACE — vii

INTRODUCTION — ix

1. PURSUE PERSONAL HEALTH — 1
2. EDUCATE YOURSELF — 27
3. PRACTICE COMMUNICATION — 57
4. FOSTER CONNECTION — 75
5. BE READY AT ANY TIME — 99
6. WELCOME QUESTIONS — 117
7. TRAIN NOT SHAME OR PUNISH — 137
8. FOCUS ON GROWTH NOT PERFECTION — 157
9. KEEP MODELING — 185
10. NEVER TURN AWAY — 209

CONCLUSION — 223

NEXT STEPS — 225

APPENDIX — 227

PREFACE

For some of you, this book might challenge your paradigms and, from time to time, it's helpful to get kicked in the paradigm.

The purpose of this book is to be a practical resource for individuals, parents and groups. It is a template for ongoing education, communication, and growth in the area of healthy sexuality. Rodney and I believe this book offers practical information that will not only benefit you who read it, but potentially your families and communities as well.

Why this book? There is a tremendous need for clear communication about healthy sexuality. The mismanagement of sexuality is so prevalent in our world, that understanding what is good and healthy about our sexuality is a better place to start. As parents, we have the opportunity to provide for our children a healthier pathway forward than many of us were given.

As parents, faith communities, and culturally, we haven't always done this well. Rodney and I believe there's a need for a new conversation.

Rodney's passion for this book came from insight and experience stemming from navigating his own personal recovery in this area and through serving as an educator, pastor, and couples facilitator for the past twenty years. It has been developed through years of parenting and couples workshops Rodney and I have led. Our emphasis on training parents was born out of seeing the need and desire many parents had to be equipped and better able to communicate with their kids in the area of sexuality.

RODNEY AND TRACI WRIGHT

Our collaboration for the book comes from 30 years of marriage, co-parenting, and our personal experience with recovery in the area of sexual addiction and helping others. It is a representation of our combined experiences and perspectives.

This book can be used individually—answering the chapter questions and the practical application—but it's best intention is to be experienced in community, with a spouse, friend, and/or small group.

We hope you are impacted by our story.

Traci

INTRODUCTION

Most parents dread the conversation. Talking about sex makes us squirm and we often avoid the topic, especially with our kids. The primary thing most parents think is, *I want to handle this differently than my parents*, but most of us don't have the framework to navigate this tough topic.

There are so many questions that come to mind when we think about how and where to begin:

- When do I start this conversation?
- How do I begin the conversation?
- Do they bring it up?
- Do I bring it up?
- How can I talk to my kids about this when I've made mistakes in this area?
- How much of my unhealthy sexual history do I share with my kids?
- Do I share it at all? If so, when and how do I share it?
- Have I found healing from my own sexual brokenness or the wounds I have received from others?
- Who can I talk with about this subject?
- Who decides what is healthy and what is unhealthy?
- From where do I derive my sexual morals?

And the list goes on and on!

This book is focused on helping parents learn how to communicate about healthy sexuality with their children. This is more than a one-time conversation, or "the birds and the bees" talk. Fostering healthy sexuality in our children requires multiple conversations, often at unexpected times, over many years. This isn't about the "one talk," but rather about opening up an ongoing dialogue that will continue to develop and mature into intimate and deep connections and healthy relationships throughout life. It's a new kind of conversation.

Our sexuality is an amazing gift; one that I believe reflects the very character and nature of our Creator—in whose image we are made. Our sexuality is deeply connected to who we are: male and female. It's the core of our spirituality—some of the deepest places of our lives. Out of this very gift and act, we have the ability to recreate, like our Creator. It's a sacred space.

As parents, we want our child's first understanding of sexuality to be that it is good. It is from God. It is positive. As I often say, "Thank God for sex!" It was His design.

If understood and managed correctly, our sexuality can be the source of some of life's greatest joys and blessings—Heaven on earth! If not understood correctly or mismanaged, it has the potential to be the cause of some of life's deepest wounds and greatest sorrows, truly creating a living hell here and now! God's idea for sex was about something good.

Whether you come from a faith or religious background, or find yourself unsure about the whole "God" thing, this book will be beneficial. For some of you, this book will encourage and reinforce you are on a good path—providing more tools and skills to improve communication and connection with your kids. For others, this may offer fresh perspective on how and when to begin these crucial conversations.

INTRODUCTION

Dignity of humanity, mutual respect for one another, and how we communicate this shows care and other-centered, self-giving love, which is the nature of God—having someone else's best interest in mind. We're called to love ourselves and love each other. What does it look like to communicate dignity and honor to others? It is embracing the intrinsic worth of every human being.

I now recognize the need not to train kids, but to train us as parents—to equip us. For all of us, what we have to contribute to our kids' lives doesn't just happen. It comes from investing ourselves in personal work and learning from others.

In this book, Traci and I are building a framework that will give you perspectives, tools, and language that are very practical and applicable. When you get to the end of this book, you will have a better starting point and feel more equipped to help your kids.

The chapters provide 10 principles and essential truths:

1. Pursue Personal Health
2. Educate Yourself
3. Practice Communication
4. Foster Connection
5. Be Ready At Any Time
6. Welcome Questions
7. Train Not Shame Or Punish
8. Focus on Growth Not Perfection
9. Keep Modeling
10. Never Turn Away

I hope you find this book meaningful and insightful. I hope it makes you laugh and makes you cry—awakening something deep within you for a better way!

My desire is that these truths will begin to transform the way you think, feel, act, and communicate about sexuality.

Rodney

CHAPTER 1

PURSUE PERSONAL HEALTH

Our personal health is one of the best gifts we can give our kids. Here is a good starting point for this book: *the best way to help our kids is to first help ourselves!* In reality, the only person we can really change is ourselves. We must realize that we are limited in helping our kids if we haven't come to terms with our own sexual history—both positive and negative—understanding it, healing from it, sharing it, and embracing it as part of our story. We are affected in so many ways: by our religious training and upbringing, communication with our family in this area, and the type or amount of education we received about our sexuality. Addiction, pornography, abortion, abuse, betrayal, and affairs may also be a part of our story. Healing our wounds and not living in shame are crucial steps as we seek to help our kids.

REGARDLESS OF OUR AGE OR STAGE OF LIFE AS A PARENT, WHEN OUR KIDS SEE US CONTINUING TO GROW AND MATURE, IT CAN HAVE A PROFOUND IMPACT ON THEM.

Many of us have heard the expression "You're only young once, but you can be immature for your whole life." An interesting thing about maturity is that it doesn't just come with age. Part of maturing is doing the deep work of our soul, so that we have something to pass on to others. At whatever level we have experienced trauma, usually it starts from our growing up years. Whether we experienced a rigid household, neglect, some type of abuse, being ignored or made fun of at school, struggling to fit in, all of us are affected by the big and small traumas of our life.

Over the years, I've had the privilege of counseling over 300 couples in the areas of pre-marriage, marital communication and conflict resolution, and parent and family issues. The relationships that transformed the most happened when individuals focused on changing themselves and not their spouse or children. Sometimes there were circumstances that forced them to seek counseling. Sometimes, on their own, they recognized they needed help. This isn't always easy. We generally have a lot of walls and defense mechanisms that can keep us from getting help. While our brain is constantly working to keep us "safe," it can often develop some extreme measures of self-protection.

Michael Dye, author of *The Genesis Process*, refers to these walls and defense mechanisms as characteristics of a Protective Personality.[1] Protective Personalities cause us to wear masks—masks we created, usually because of fear and trauma, and used at some point in our life, but now they are keeping us from allowing people into our lives at a deeper level. Wearing masks can seem so natural that we're often not even aware of it, unless someone points it out or we begin the process of personal recovery.

Recovery involves moving toward the things we are afraid of. It is participating in what the Spirit is doing within our lives.[2] Recovery is not just for the alcoholic or sex addict. Recovery

---

[1] Dye, M. (2012). *The Genesis Process: For Change Groups, Book 1 and 2, Individual Workbook* (4th ed.). Auburn, CA: Michael Dye. 109.

[2] Ibid. 2.

CHAPTER 1: PURSUE PERSONAL HEALTH

is for everyone who is human. Recovery means to return to a normal state of health, mind, or strength. Isn't this what our spiritual journey is about? The word for save or salvation in the Bible, the Greek word Sozo, is about restoration:

FOR THE SON OF MAN HAS COME TO SEEK AND TO SAVE THAT WHICH WAS LOST.[3]

It has been translated as heals, restores, makes whole.[4]

Here are some examples of people I have worked with over the years who looked at their own health in order to move into healthier relationships with others:

- A young woman was date raped in college and shared openly in pre-marriage counseling that she was getting help from a therapist to process this traumatic experience. She wanted to move into her new marriage yet realized this negative sexual experience could very well create challenges in her marriage relationship. She had the courage to talk about it and seek help.
- A retired 65-year-old father who was a workaholic, but learned how to slow down and be emotionally available for his family.
- A 76-year-old married man who was abused by a priest as a young boy and has spent his life struggling with same-sex hookups. He joined a recovery group and began working through his brokenness. I said to him, "I'm glad you're getting help at 76, because it's really hard work at

---

[3] Luke 19:10 NASB

[4] Bible Study Tools (2019). Retrieved from https://www.biblestudytools.com/lexicons/greek/nas/sozo.html.

86, and at 96, it's nearly impossible!" The point being, "It is never too late to start your healing journey."

- A young woman who was highly successful in her career, but realized her alcohol use was getting out of hand, so sought help in a local AA group.
- The many young couples who are trying to figure out their own sexual relationship in marriage. They are seeking help through counseling or a support group, so they will have something to offer their kids.

Or, in my case, seeking help in my mid-20s, as a young husband and father, because I needed retraining from years of sexual addiction.

Each one of these stories represents a person(s) who decided not to let their painful past or destructive behavior remain a secret and keep them trapped. They chose to get help. Recognizing we need help involves taking a risk and opening up our lives to others.

AS SICK AS OUR SECRETS

We are as sick as our secrets.[5] Sometimes the secret is abuse. Sometimes the secret is abortion. Sometimes the secret is, fill in the blank: loss of our virginity, had an affair, had a pattern of sexual or relationship addiction, or any type of promiscuity. This becomes part of the secrets we carry. We think, *If others really knew me they would not love and accept me. They wouldn't! They would reject me*, so our secrets go underground. This was part of my story.

My struggle with pornography started as a young boy and I think my story is fairly common. Raised in a conservative

---

[5] Smith, B. & Wilson, B. (1939). *The Big Book of Alcoholics Anonymous.* Asheville, NC: Lark Publishing LLC.

CHAPTER 1: PURSUE PERSONAL HEALTH

Christian home, my father was a pastor at a large church. I am the youngest of five children, and I was born when my parents were around 40 years old. If I could describe my dad, who is in his 90s today, I would say he is a cross between Billy Graham and Ronald Reagan, and throw in 10 percent John Wayne—that's my dad. I didn't think this guy ever made a mistake. In fact, when I was 16 years old, I said to my mother, "Has Dad ever sinned?" My mom replied, "Oh hon, I assure you. Your father has sinned."

Talking about sexuality was not something that was comfortable in our family or faith community. It was not a part of our conversation. So when I was exposed to pornography as a young boy, I didn't know how to manage or talk about it. I thought that somehow all of my normal sexual development as a human being was bad and evil—which it isn't—but if it gets connected to something distorted, it can really be destructive.

So as a young person, I was in church, youth choir, going on missions trips—I spent a lot of time praying at an altar asking God to take my problem away, so heavy with guilt—trying to do all the right things, and still struggling. Whenever I went to youth group, I would pray, "God, you know I don't want to do this any more, so I want You to help me," but I continued to struggle.

My parents were very loving, but I didn't always feel safe to be honest with them about my mistakes and difficulties. I didn't have the framework to say, "Hey Dad, I saw..." or "Mom, I experienced..." This contributed to my addictive cycle. Today, I realize how internalizing my behavior became a way of coping with my challenges of pornography and masturbation. Looking back, I didn't realize the addictive pattern that was forming in my life. Now, I understand that what I was experiencing as a kid was the binge-purge cycle of addiction. This led me down some dark roads and to some painful experiences. I didn't understand that my behavior was an addiction or find help until much later in life.

Eventually, I thought I should probably talk to someone about my sexual struggles, so I confessed to my brother, Ryan, who I saw as a very safe person. Being 20 months older than me, he didn't have all of the tools to help me, but this was the beginning of it not being a secret. Even though I now had confession and accountability, I wasn't transforming.

I went to Bible college in the deep South, in the 80s, at a school that was started by a famous TV evangelist. He traveled the world, filling stadiums with 100,000 people and sharing the gospel—it was about saying a specific prayer so the Divine wouldn't send you to hell when you died. It seemed more focused on being transactional than transformational or relational—fear-based—and what I would refer to as selling hell insurance. Meanwhile, he was caught living in his own personal hell of sexual addiction.

I was there when he shared in front of his congregation of 7,000 and the whole world through the media. This was a big deal! To some, he was like the protestant pope. It affected a lot of people and challenged our belief systems. He, like myself, had been struggling with this for years and his faith hadn't transformed him. It was an opportunity for something to change. The whole world was listening. I was a young adult, sitting in the balcony with my girlfriend, Traci, who is now my wife, and thinking: *Hey, you're not the only one. Help us out of the ditch.*

I was hoping that this would change culture, and the conversation would open up, but it just went away. At this time, it wasn't safe to be real and vulnerable. This was an opportunity for church culture to embrace change, but nothing really changed.

I continued to struggle with porn and masturbation. As a young man I believed if I had a sexual problem, I should get

CHAPTER 1: PURSUE PERSONAL HEALTH

married. We all know that "marriage fixes everything," right? Actually, those of us who are married know that's not true. Marriage doesn't change us—it just reveals more of what it finds. **IF YOU'RE HEALTHY GOING INTO MARRIAGE, GUESS WHAT MARRIAGE IS GOING TO REVEAL? YOUR HEALTH. IF YOU'RE UNHEALTHY GOING INTO MARRIAGE, IT'S GOING TO REVEAL YOUR UNHEALTH.** So, I went into marriage unhealthy in this area and the pattern continued.

My heart desired one thing, but my actions displayed another. Romans 7 describes this perfectly. "I do not understand what I do. For what I want to do, I do not do, but what I hate I do..." I realized there were parts of me that were incongruent—that needed to be integrated into the rest of my life.

I was a pastor in a church. I was happily married. I had confessed to my brother, and my dad, and I still wasn't transforming. I said to God, "I don't even know if you're real. Maybe this faith thing works for others, but not for me."

I was sitting in a church service and prayed this simple prayer: "God, please lead me to people and resources that can help me." I heard the Spirit say, *That drummer is going to lead you to healing.* I thought, *Not that guy, he's a sexual trauma assessment treatment therapist. If I go see him, that means I'm messed up.* I felt like the Spirit said, *Yep, that's right. You're messed up. We—Father, Son, and Spirit—fully anticipated your struggle, Rodney.*

With this therapist, I started a three-year process. I worked through Dr. Patrick Carnes book for sexual addiction, *Out of the Shadows.*[6] This was the beginning of my transformation. Dr. Carnes, who is a leading expert in the area of sexual addiction,

---

[6] Carnes, P. (2001). *Out of the Shadows: Understanding Sexual Addiction* (3rd ed.) City Center, MN: Hazelden.

suggests that pornography use isn't just a moral issue, it's a brain issue. I learned how to integrate my faith, my emotions, and some of my early traumas...and my sexuality.

As a boy, I thought that repentance was about telling God how sorry you were. If I was sorry enough and tipped the repent-o-meter, God would dole out some forgiveness and I would be changed.

I see repentance differently now, as a process, as a way of changing how we think, and more than a one-time experience. The word for repentance is *Metanoia*, sometimes translated "changing our thinking" or you might say "to repent" is to "change the way you think."

With help, I was able to disclose to my wife and completely let go of my secret, and years later, to share with my children.

This is a common story. Actually, statistics say that many men and women from a more rigid or rules-based home will be more susceptible to pornography.[7] Even those who are conservative and may be following the rules in many other ways, like I was, can be pulled into negative choices in this area of life. There are often pieces of religious homes and communities that are just not helpful. It may even set us up for failure because we don't think it's safe to be honest and open about our struggles.

After speaking and sharing some of my story, it's amazing how many people tell me about their struggle with addiction or how they were abused or hurt by the sexual sin of another person—and they have never told anyone. These are the secrets people often carry their entire lives.

We can only be a healthy person if we have intimacy in our lives. Sexual intimacy is one part of intimacy, but intimacy is

---

[7] Carnes, P. (2015). *Facing the Shadows: Starting Sexual and Relationship Recovery* (3rd ed.) Carefree, AZ: Gentle Path Press.

not about being sexual. Intimacy is about knowing and being known: "Into-Me-You-See."[8] To experience intimacy means to truly be seen by another. To take it a step further, it is not only to be seen, but accepted.

I find that fear and shame are what keep us most trapped from sharing our lives. This creates the negative thought, *If I share with you, and you know all my pain and struggles, you won't love and accept me.* When we are involved in a safe community, what we find is the opposite. A grace-filled, safe community will be the very thing that frees our soul. Why does this happen? I believe it's because we are made in the image of God, and God is a relational being. The Trinity—the Father, Son, and Holy Spirit—are in relationship with one another. They invite us to participate in this relationship and model what it looks like to "mutually submit" to each other.[9] The beauty of the Trinity is their intimacy—knowing and being known.

> NOW THIS IS ETERNAL LIFE: THAT THEY KNOW YOU, THE ONLY TRUE GOD, AND JESUS CHRIST, WHOM YOU HAVE SENT.[10]

We might have a heart to help our children, but think, *I have made so many mistakes. I can't go back and change this. In fact, I don't even want to look at it. I want to keep it buried. Or, I just want to move forward and ignore it, hoping it goes away. There's no hope for me, but I want to help my children.*

---

[8] Riemersma, J. (2019). Pastoral Sex Addiction Professional (PSAP) Training. International Institute for Trauma & Addiction Professionals. February.

[9] Ephesians 5:21

[10] John 17:3

You can't move forward from your past while it still has its claws in you.[11] At some point you have to turn around and, with the help of others, start to face and heal from your past. I'm here to tell you that your own health will be the greatest gift you give your children. It is very hard to lead the way when you're wrapped up in your own shame.

> WHEN WE DENY OUR STORIES, THEY DEFINE US. WHEN WE OWN OUR STORIES, WE GET TO WRITE A BRAVE NEW ENDING.[12]

SHAME

We usually have to start with the shame that surrounds this area of our life. Whether it was something done to us or mistakes of our own, if we can't come to terms with shame and open up in a safe environment, we cannot begin to heal. We have to feel to heal.[13] Many people have bottled up their feelings and emotions for so long—or they are living in denial—that they are not aware of or in touch with their feelings. This is foundational to healing shame: learning to identify what we are feeling.

EVEN IF WE DON'T HAVE A LOT OF SHAME SURROUNDING OUR SEXUALITY, AND WE HAVE MADE GOOD CHOICES IN THIS AREA, OUR OWN HOLISTIC HEALTH IS GOING TO BE A HUGE PART OF UNDERSTANDING AND HELPING OUR CHILDREN. They may or may not process life and walk through adolescence the same way we did. A humble approach—at their

---

[11] This is a quote that my therapist, Jesse Watson, used to say to me.

[12] Brown, B. (2015). *Rising Strong*. Houston, TX: The Daring Way.

[13] Dye, M. (2012). *The Genesis Process: For Change Groups, Book 1 and 2, Individual Workbook* (4th ed.). Auburn, CA: Michael Dye.

level, sharing whatever areas of our lives we have experienced failure or shame—will go a long way and allow our personal healing to bring health to our family.

From the beginning, in the story of Creation, when Adam and Eve made a mistake, they hid. They were afraid of God. The incarnation of Christ is God becoming human to help us see that He is trying to heal us from the deception of sin, not judge or hurt us. **God's judgment is always toward the things in our lives that are hurting us.** He is trying to destroy the lies that deceive us, not judge or punish us.

There is another way of looking at this story of Adam and Eve that is not about punishment. Christ was consistently confirming the true heart of the Father toward us. If we isolate from God and others during times of pressure, we follow the example of Adam and Eve, who hid from God in the garden.

Shame is connected to fear. There is no fear in love. Perfect love casts out fear.[14] What's broken in us—our shame and fear—contributes to or adds to what becomes broken in our children. If we become a healthy parent, it helps to correct this pattern. We do this by understanding what is most true and then passing it on to our children.

Unfortunately, in our broken world, we sometimes pass along our false beliefs and skewed perspectives to our children.

---

[14] 1 John 4:18

In his book, *Anatomy of the Soul*, Curt Thompson shares:

IN FACT, THE STORY OF EDEN SHOWS HOW, LIKE ADAM AND EVE, WE ARE MORE INTERESTED IN KNOWING RIGHT FROM WRONG (A DOMINANTLY LEFT-BRAINED HEMISPHERE FUNCTION USED TO COPE WITH FEAR AND SHAME) THAN KNOWING GOD, WHICH REQUIRES THE INTEGRATION OF ALL PARTS OF THE BRAIN.[15]

This is about knowing God not just knowing about God.

HOLISTIC SPIRITUALITY

As a child, my faith upbringing put a lot of emphasis on the dos and don'ts when growing our "spiritual life." This included time spent reading the Bible, personal prayer, attending weekend services, and witnessing about Christ to others. All of these are good things, don't misunderstand me, but if these things are the "spiritual part" then other things could seem non spiritual or not as important. As if to say, "These things really matter to God" more than the other areas of our lives.

In looking at our life, we tend to segregate spirituality as one piece of the whole. For example, we may divide our life into several categories, such as mental, emotional, relational, sexual, and spiritual segments as we see in the following graph. The spiritual is just *a part* of the whole.

---

[15] Thompson, C. (2010). *Anatomy of the Soul: Surprising connections between neuroscience and spiritual practices that can transform you life and relationships.* Carol Stream, IL: Tyndale House Publishers, Inc.

CHAPTER 1: PURSUE PERSONAL HEALTH

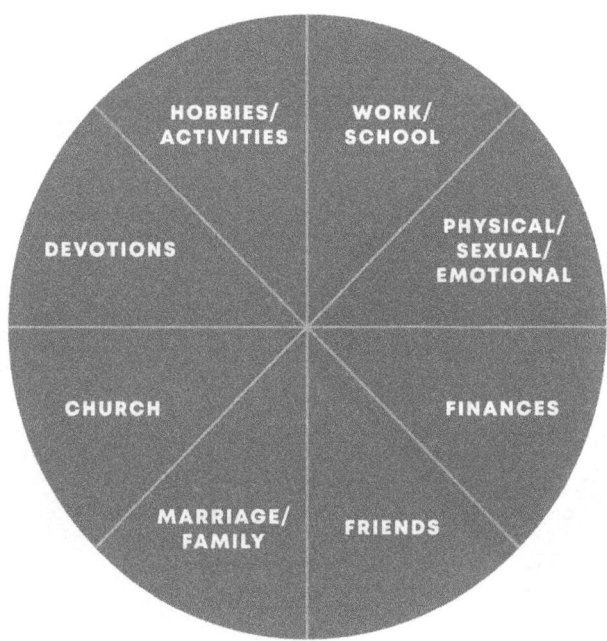

I no longer believe that spirituality is a separate part of our life, one piece of the puzzle, but **spirituality is the integration of truth into all areas of our life**. The following diagrams show both the segregated and integrated way of seeing our spirituality.

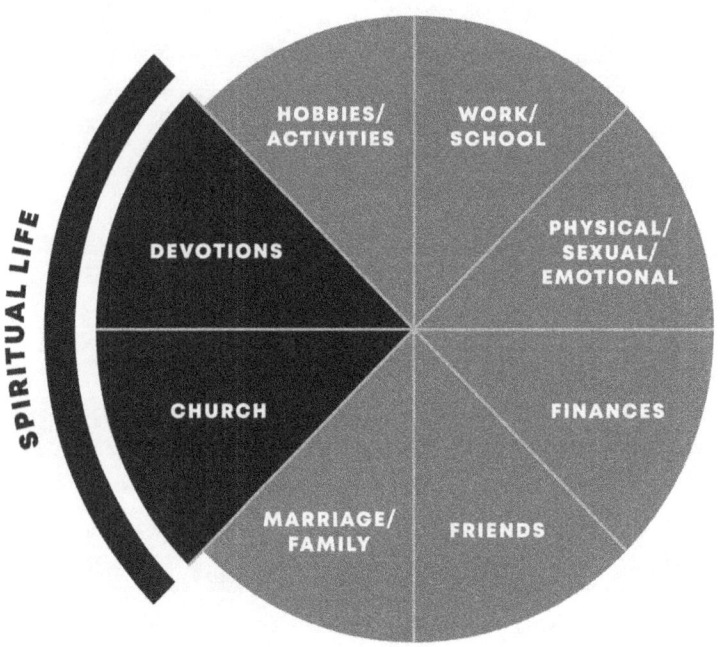

I've heard it said that in the first century Jewish mind, which Jesus lived in, they saw all of life as a sacred gift or act of worship unto God.[16] It wasn't segregated. Health in all areas was seen as important and spiritual. Colossians 3:17 says, "And whatever you do, whether in word or deed, do it all in the name of the Lord Jesus..." In His day and culture, if we were to ask Jesus, "How is your spiritual life?" He may have responded with the statement: all of life is spiritual.

---

[16] Bell, R. (2007). *Everything is Spiritual* [DVD]. United States: Zondervan.

CHAPTER 1: PURSUE PERSONAL HEALTH

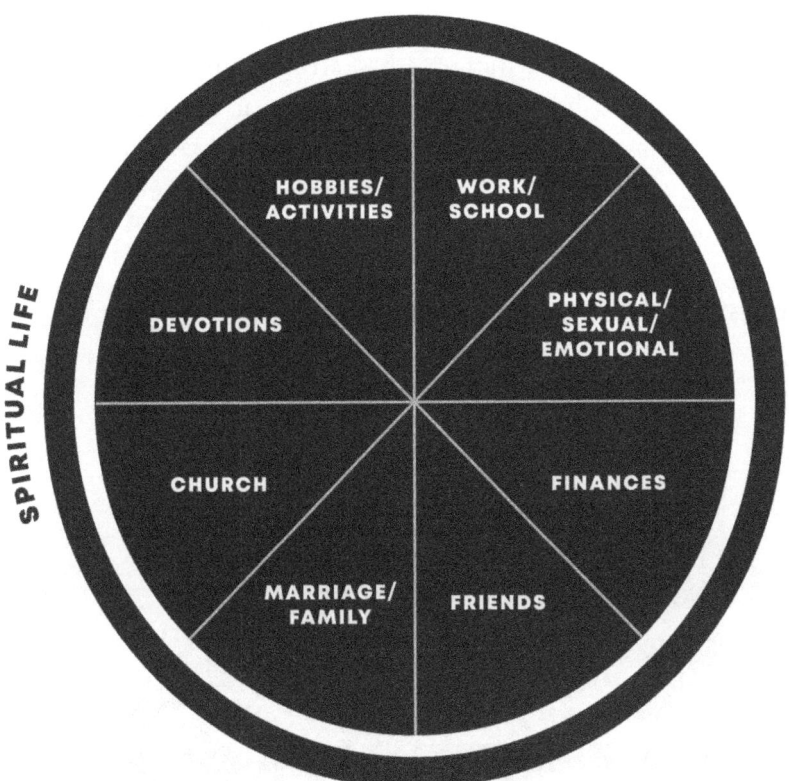

This requires seeing ourselves as holistic or interconnected beings. Without this perspective, we don't know how to integrate our spirituality into all areas of our life. This helps us understand how many people can attend church, pray, read their Bible daily, and still struggle with sexual promiscuity, addiction, and shame, as I did. This same concept goes beyond the area of our sexuality into incongruency in all areas of relationships, whether unforgiveness, selfishness, or pride, or any number of things. This is one of the reasons I believe we are all in recovery.

Finding health in every part of our life matters and it's all connected. This is how holistic spirituality is developed.

Continuing on a path of recovery throughout my life is what has helped me. Even though I first worked through my sexual brokenness and health over 20 years ago, it has led me to an understanding of what real recovery looks like—continually integrating God into all areas of my life—including all my past pain and trauma.

GRIEVING TRAUMA AND LOSSES

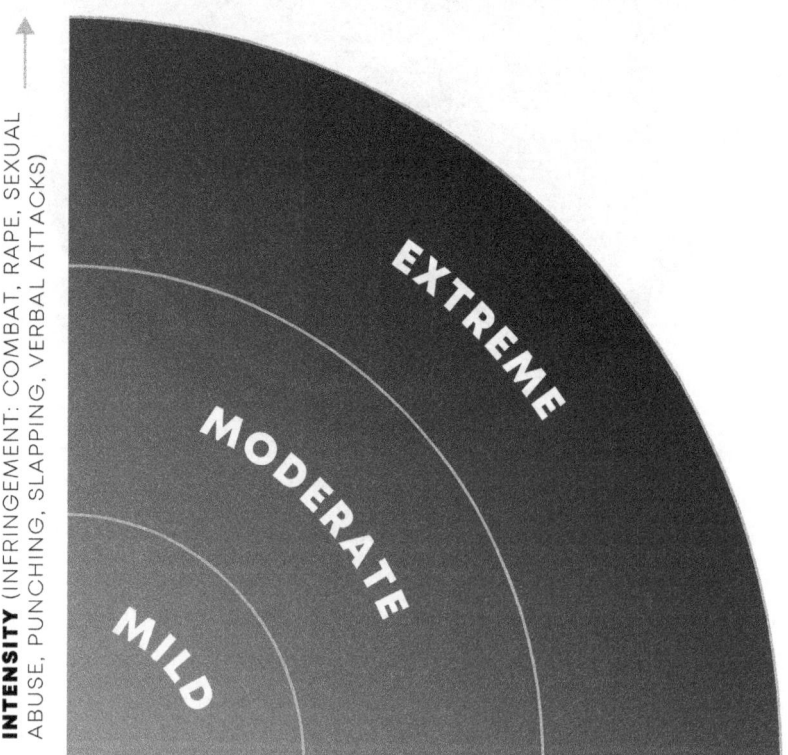

CHAPTER 1: PURSUE PERSONAL HEALTH

Many times, our addictions, sexual misuse, and negative patterns come from trauma or losses in our life that we don't know how to grieve. Nothing goes away until it is resolved.[17]

Trauma comes in many forms, sometimes referred to as *Big T* trauma, like sexual or physical abuse, or multiple *Little t* trauma, like being teased or rejected.[18] Big T trauma—usually one-time experiences—are significant and affect us in many ways. This could include military experience, a tragic accident, or being the victim of rape, sexual assault, or other violent experiences.

Little t trauma—reoccurring experiences—are significant because of the messages they carry.[19] It could either be the message someone told us or the message we took away from the experiences. For instance, when I made mistakes in the area of sexuality, I believed this was the most shameful thing I could do. Because no one talked about it, and I believed all of my sexual feelings were lust, I attached a message to my trauma: *I am damaged for the rest of my life. I'm irreparable.* As a young man planning to be a minister and help others, I thought the Divine clearly made a mistake in me. I even thought at times, *God wasted a draft pick on me.*

Our trauma has to be grieved in order for us to move forward in our healing. **OUR GRIEF ISN'T WHAT'S WRONG WITH US—OUR GRIEF IS ACTUALLY WHAT'S RIGHT WITH US.**[20] Grief work is some of the hardest work we do. This is

---

[17] Hickman, A. (2019). Pastoral Sex Addiction Professional (PSAP) Training. International Institute for Trauma & Addiction Professionals. February.

[18] Shapiro, F. (2001). *Eye Movement Desensitization and Reprocessing: Basic Principles, Protocols, and Procedures* (2nd ed.). New York: NY; The Guilford Press.

[19] Hickman, A. (2019). Pastoral Sex Addiction Professional (PSAP) Training. International Institute for Trauma & Addiction Professionals. February.

[20] Petrie, J. (2019). One to Another. Retrieved from http://www.onetoanother.org/.

why it is often avoided. If we're not taught how to process grief and let go of pain, and this life can definitely be painful, we internalize our pain and stay stuck. This can greatly affect our relationship with ourselves and others. We have to learn how to process our pain, be honest about it, and talk about what hurts us. One of the most important gifts we can give to our kids and families is to provide a safe place to share our losses, fears, and feelings.

If this is a foreign concept to you, you may want to start by taking a grief class or looking for another type of support group where you can share openly. I have been involved in grief classes and support in our community for many years. Many people have also sought help with a therapist or local counselor who provides a nonjudgmental space to let go of grief.

I am part of Pure Desire Ministries, an organization that supports recovery groups specializing in the areas of sexual addiction and betrayal. A large part of this process is dealing with our trauma and releasing grief. All good recovery groups for sexual addiction, or otherwise, will point us toward grieving our losses. Most addictions are coping mechanisms for the trauma and losses we have not grieved.

REGRETS NOT GRIEVED TURN INTO SHAME.[21] Many times we haven't grieved our regrets because we aren't willing to face them. (I will talk more about shame in Chapter 7). We are sometimes afraid, *If I open up that box, I might never recover.* Or, *If I start to cry and grieve that loss, I may never stop crying.*[22] Continuing to minimize or deny the deep losses of our life, keeping them underground and internalized, is what hurts us the most. Our

---

[21] Paul Young. He shared this at a conference I attended.
[22] Petrie, J. (2019). One to Another. Grief Release. Retrieved from http://www.onetoanother.org/.

CHAPTER 1: PURSUE PERSONAL HEALTH

pain and trauma has to be finished—it has to be processed.[23] It has to be grieved.

In other words, our history affects us! If our history is negative and we don't have healthy people or a healthy understanding of how to process it correctly, it will not only impact our lives but the lives of our children.

If you're struggling with addiction right now or carrying a painful secret, don't necessarily go home and confess. Seek help with processing and disclosing your addiction with a trained professional or a recovery group. We all need to own it and share it with at least one other safe person who can help us work through it.

SAFE PEOPLE

Sometimes, if we have been betrayed by others or grew up without many safe relationships, opening up seems like the last thing we want to do. If we grew up in an environment where it wasn't safe to share our thoughts and feelings, we may simply not know how. Two very influential and well-known books in the area of recovery are *Boundaries*[24] and *Safe People*[25] by Henry Cloud and John Townsend. They do a great job looking at these two crucial and foundational areas of our lives.

If you struggle with setting personal boundaries or knowing how to develop safe relationships in your life, or know others

---

[23] Hickman, A. (2019). Pastoral Sex Addiction Professional (PSAP) Training. International Institute for Trauma & Addiction Professionals. February.

[24] Cloud, H. & Townsend, J. (1992). *Boundaries: When to say yes, how to say no to take control of your life*. Grand Rapids, MI: Zondervan.

[25] Cloud, H. & Townsend, J. (1995). *Safe People: How to Find Relationships That Are Good for You and Avoid Those That Aren't*. Grand Rapids, MI: Zondervan.

who struggle in this area, these books are a good place to start. If you aren't sure how healthy you are in these areas—setting healthy boundaries and knowing what safe people look like—ask someone you trust for their opinion.

We all need a trusted friend who will be honest with us.

DON'T TALK. DON'T TRUST. DON'T FEEL.

All families have some level of dysfunction. ==BY THE VERY NATURE OF BEING HUMAN, WE DO NOT HAVE PERFECT FAMILIES. WE PASS ALONG TRAITS TO OUR CHILDREN SOMETIMES WITHOUT EVEN NOTICING.==

Dysfunctional families have unwritten rules.[26] It is helpful to be aware of this and understand how our family of origin may have passed some of these unwritten rules on to us, but also how we may do this ourselves.

1. DON'T TALK.

Don't talk about what is actually going on in the family, whether with each other or outside of the family. It creates a sense of denial around what is really going on and sends a strong message to *act like everything is fine and make sure everyone else thinks we are a perfectly normal family.*

Issues such as substance abuse, physical or sexual abuse, or emotional abuse—showing up as uncontrolled anger, criticism and belittling—get swept under the rug. No one is acknowledging or facing the family problems, so family members aren't able to reach out and be honest, with each other or outsiders, to get help and to heal. Honesty and trust are a basis for healthy connected relationships.

---

[26] Black, C. (1987). *"It Will Never Happen To Me" Children of Alcoholics: As Youngsters—Adolescents—Adults.* New York, NY: Ballantine Books.

CHAPTER 1: PURSUE PERSONAL HEALTH

2. DON'T TRUST.

Parents are the "big people" in our world, who we are dependent on as children. We believe that we should be able to depend on them to meet our physical and emotional needs, but when they are undependable or inconsistent in meeting those needs, we learn not to trust them. This can be through neglect, emotional absence, broken promises, and disappointments. The parent may show care for their children, but also are consistently preoccupied with their own issues or the issues of another family member.

When we don't trust those in our family, the world can become a scary place, we become anxious and insecure, and will have an underlying sense of mistrust for others. Inconsistent emotional support teaches us that we can't count on others. This keeps us isolated from being able to ask for help and develop strong bonds with others, and we expect to have to meet our needs by ourselves. We learn that we cannot depend on our parents to meet our needs, so we learn to ignore these needs and find our own coping mechanisms to anesthetize the pain.

3. DON'T FEEL.

The message *don't feel* teaches us that our emotions are not welcome. We witness our parents using their unhealthy coping behaviors rather than expressing their emotions in a healthy way, and we learn to do the same. We get very comfortable with hiding our emotions and create our own numbing devices. If we do share an emotion, we may be ignored, shamed, or punished, so we quickly realize that **expressing emotions is not welcome**. Unhealthy parents may justify or minimize what we are experiencing. We may be told that something isn't a big deal, when it actually is. Our feelings may not be validated. When we learn to deny our feelings over a long period of time, it can be a pattern that lasts into adulthood. If we need to shut out the pain of being hurt and disconnected, we learn to shut down other emotions as well.

Being aware of the unwritten rules in a dysfunctional family allows us to be able to do something positive about it in our own family. For example, learning to be open and honest about our own feelings, so we can train and model this to our children. We have the opportunity to begin now with open, age-appropriate conversations with our kids about their thoughts, feelings, and sexuality. Being a healthy parent means our children will be able to trust us—this is the beginning of them learning to trust other safe adults and the world around them as they grow.

If we are developing consistency for them and they are generally able to count on us, it builds the trust that is needed. This happens when we, as parents, develop an awareness of our own feelings and learn how to express our feelings. This isn't something that comes naturally to a lot of us, but identifying and naming, out loud, to others what we are feeling is a powerful tool in our own health and a powerful model to our children.

It is in relationships that we are hurt or wounded, and it is in relationships that we must heal.[27] Allowing other human beings into our deepest hurts is where the healing begins. When we are able to experience love and acceptance after opening up, we begin to change our "thinking errors"—our internal messages that tell us we are unlovable and unworthy of acceptance and belonging.

I have seen this time and time again, as men in my groups open up and allow themselves to see what it looks like to be vulnerable and let other men into their lives. My wife has worked with

---

[27] Dye, M. (2012). *The Genesis Process: For Change Groups, Book 1 and 2, Individual Workbook* (4th ed.). Auburn, CA: Michael Dye.

CHAPTER 1: PURSUE PERSONAL HEALTH

women struggling with substance and non substance-behavioral addiction recovery and has witnessed the same response.

Healing typically happens slowly, painfully, incrementally, but always relationally.[28] You can be sorrowful, but if you don't see your thinking error, it is hard to change (to repent) when you don't see where you are getting it wrong regarding self, God, and others. You can be sorrowful about your behavior, but you need those around you who are able to help you identify your false beliefs and walk alongside you in the process of change.

It's amazing how opening up our lives to others shows us that we are so much more alike on a human level than we might think. This often involves great risk, but the payoff is incredible.

YOU'RE WORTH IT

In October 2017, a young man invited me to breakfast. I met him on the way home from a hunting trip in the woods of North Idaho. This young man had been a friend of my kids for many years and had recently started dating my daughter. During breakfast, he showed me a picture of a diamond ring on his iPhone and said, "I'd like to give this to your daughter, but before I do, I want to ask you for her hand in marriage."

As a father, this is one of those conversations you anticipate having someday. It's a time when most dads want to emphasize to the young man the responsibility of cherishing their daughter. Sometimes this can come out as, "You better not hurt her, or else." I've even heard one father say, "If you hurt my daughter, I know people, and it won't go well for you."

---

[28] Author Paul Young shared this in a service I attended and believe it to be true from my own experience.

I didn't want to take the approach of motivating my potential son-in-law out of fear. I wanted him to start with his own value. I said to him, "Daniel, if you love and value yourself well, you will have no problem loving and valuing my daughter." I also told him, "If you ever lose sight of your worth and value, may I be one of the first people you call to help remind you."

This is not only true for Daniel, but for all of us. This is our starting point—whether going into marriage, beginning a family, or training our kids.

WHEREVER YOU'RE AT IN THE PROCESS, AND REGARDLESS OF YOUR AGE OR SEASON OF LIFE, YOUR PERSONAL HEALTH IS FIRST PRIORITY.

Learning and growing is a part of our development as humans. When it comes to our sexuality and the management of it, this is true as well. I didn't always believe this, but I do now. This is one of the best gifts we can give our kids—to work through our own personal history!

Here's what I want you to take away: **healthy people seek help. Seeking help is not a sign of our weakness, it's a sign of our wisdom.**

Let this become your mantra. You are worth getting help. Let that settle deep in your heart. You are worth it!

CHAPTER 1
TRY THIS!

IDENTIFY AND REACH OUT TO A HEALTHY TRUSTED PERSON OR GROUP FOR SUPPORT THIS WEEK.

OR

IDENTIFY AND TAKE ONE SMALL STEP TOWARD PERSONAL HEALTH THIS WEEK.

QUESTIONS

1 | What have you done in your life to invest in your personal health?

2 | Do you think seeking help is a sign of weakness or strength? Why or why not?

3 | What prevents us from becoming personally healthy in the area of sexuality?

4 | Why is it so important to look at your personal health first in this area?

5 | Briefly share a time when you stepped out and sought help. Was it a positive or negative experience?

CHAPTER 2

EDUCATE YOURSELF

How *do* we learn and how *should* we learn about our sexuality? There are three primary sources that shape our understanding: **our families**, **our culture**, and **our faith communities**. Of these three, I think parents should take on the primary role of educating and guiding their children in the area of sexuality. This is important, both as a responsibility and a privilege. It's the beauty of bringing our kids into the world and becoming a part of educating and instructing them—instead of expecting the faith community, school, peers, or culture to educate them, while we stay silent. **WHEN FAMILY, CULTURE, AND FAITH COMMUNITIES ARE HEALTHY AND WORK TOGETHER, IT CAN PROVIDE A GREAT ENVIRONMENT FOR KIDS TO LEARN AND LIVE OUT POSITIVE PERSPECTIVES ABOUT SEXUALITY.**

Recently, I was coming back from teaching at a Christian university in Noida, India. The college president invited me to talk with the students on the subject of healthy sexuality. I shared some of my story about struggling with pornography as a young person in college and shared some support group materials for men and women on sexual addiction. The students had come from primarily Hindi and Christian backgrounds and were mainly from Nepal, Burma, and India. Speaking on this topic is difficult to do in India because it is a honor-shame culture. In this culture, if people struggle with sexual addiction or mistakes—even if they've been wounded or abused by someone else's sexual brokenness—they can't speak publicly about it because it would bring dishonor to them and their family. I was so grateful the college was supportive of having me come and address these issues with the students.

As I started to share with the students that morning, I said, "I've come here on the invitation of your college president to share my story of dishonor, in order to lead you to a God who wants to bring honor to your life in this area." At the end of my talk, I opened it up for questions and many of the students, both male and female, were able to ask questions and share their stories. Later that day, a group of students came to me and said (through a translator), "Thank you so much for coming and speaking about this issue. It's a challenge that we all face, due to technology and the Internet, but nobody in our culture speaks about this."

When I left India to fly back to the United States, I had a layover in Dubai. While waiting at the gate between flights, the area where I was sitting started to fill up. An older couple, who were Muslim, asked if they could sit down next to me. I slid my luggage over and made a place for them to sit and introduced myself. We struck up a conversation and I learned they were on their way to Seattle for the graduation of their son, who was attending the University of Washington.

While speaking to them, a younger man approached me, in his mid-thirties, and introduced himself. He was also the son of the couple sitting next to me. I introduced myself and he asked me, "What brings you to this part of the country? Why are you here?" I said, "I'm a teacher and a counselor, and I've come to India to do some teaching at a university." He asked what I was

CHAPTER 2: EDUCATE YOURSELF

lecturing on at the school. I told him I was sharing about the life and teachings of Jesus, and how I believed He came to help all of humanity, not to start another religion.

Then, he said, "What do you counsel in?" I replied, "I counsel on addiction." He continued, "What kind of addiction?" I paused and said, "I counsel in the area of sexual addiction. I also teach parents how to help their kids in this area, because of the challenges of pornography." He said to me, "I have young kids. How would I help my kids in this area?"

I was a bit surprised at his openness, but I reached in my backpack and grabbed some teaching materials to give him. This started a great conversation about training and teaching our kids about healthy sexuality. He told me that he lives in Saudi Arabia and is a part of the Muslim faith, but the area of pornography is an area of struggle in his country and culture as well.

Before I left for India, I was talking to a business acquaintance about the reason for my trip and my own story of struggle and healing. He shared that he had struggled for many years in this area, and had recently joined a recovery group within the Mormon church where he attended.

The struggle with pornography is not just a Mormon problem, a Muslim problem, a Hindu problem, or a Christian problem. This is a human problem.

I'm going to focus on the area of pornography throughout this book, not just because it's a part of my history, but because of what the experts say: with growing technology, the pornography industry is quickly becoming the biggest influence on pop culture, on our young people, and the number one sex educator of our children.[29] Do you hear this and understand

---

[29] Dines, G. (2010). *Pornland: How Porn Has Hijacked Our Sexuality*. Boston, MA: Beacon Press.

the implications of what this means? If culture is the primary educator, then pornography—those who create pornography and their agenda—is "the primary sex educator" of our children. This influence cannot be avoided. It's free, it's accessible, and it's becoming increasingly more violent.

Pornography is a multi-billion dollar industry targeting and marketing to our kids.[30] There are teams of people sitting around a table looking for ways to get pornography into the hands and minds of our children at younger and younger ages. Some studies say that the average age of exposure is now younger than 11 years old and may be as young as seven or eight years old.[31] In my community, an elementary school counselor is dealing with second graders who are addicted to pornography.

Outside of direct pornography use, its influence has created an oversexualized, pornified culture that seeps into how we view ourselves and the roles of men and women. It has become a public health crisis and many are fighting to set limits for the sake of our kids and their futures.[32] Dr. Donald L. Hilton, a neurosurgeon who spoke at a conference I attended, stated, "This problem is affecting every family, but some may not know it yet."[33]

---

[30] Ibid.

[31] Ibid.

[32] Dines, G. (2019). Culture Reframed. Retrieved from https://www.culturereframed.org/.

[33] Oliva, A. (2019). Pornography: The New Drug. Catholic Medical Association. Spokane, WA: Gonzaga University. Retrieved from https://www.gonzaga.edu/news-events/stories/2019/2/15/porn-conference-2019.

CHAPTER 2: EDUCATE YOURSELF

FAMILIES

As families, how are we doing with educating our kids about healthy sexuality? When we think about our own family of origin, was it a safe place to ask questions and learn about sexuality? Growing up, how was sexuality talked about in our family? For some of us, it was never talked about and, for others, everything was out in the open, where there didn't seem to be any boundaries. How our families viewed sexuality and this perspective greatly influences us in one way or another.

My wife and I definitely didn't have this all figured out. We were both still healing and working on our own personal health and recovery when we were raising our kids. We've discovered from our own personal experience, and learned from others, that parents can continue to grow and influence their kids on into adulthood.

From what I've learned, here are some things healthy parents do:

- Foster deep connections with their kids regardless of their child's behavior.
- Welcome questions with their kids about sexuality.
- Set the tone for open conversation.
- Normalize what their kids are going through.
- Give age-appropriate answers to their kids' questions.
- Develop a culture of learning together in the home without shame.

Family is a place to let our kids know: it's okay to be honest. This is where you learn. We know you don't know everything, so we want this to be a place you can be open, honest, safe, and where you can talk about anything. Not only about sexuality, but any area of your life where you hurt.

The chapters in this book will dive deeper into these individual subjects as they pertain to the family.

IF WE WANT TO BE THE PRIMARY INFLUENCE IN OUR CHILDREN'S LIVES AND OF THE YOUNGER GENERATION, WE HAVE TO BE HEALTHY, EDUCATED, AND AWARE. Then, we have to be ready to share what we understand and believe in with our kids.

THINGS I'VE LEARNED

At birth, a baby boy can have an erection in the first five minutes after birth, and, in fact, we now know that baby boys can have an erection while still in the womb.[34] Some of you might be thinking, *This explains a lot about the male species, right?* But it's how males are hardwired. When referring to a newborn baby boy, no one says, "Oh my gosh, we've got a pervert here." Baby girls can vaginally lubricate within the first 24 hours after birth. Both of these examples illustrate how our sexuality is a part of who we are—from birth. This is good. It's beautiful!

We have looked at how we are made in the image of our Creator, male and female, and our sexuality is good. It is also something that has to be managed.

From the moment of birth we are sexual beings. If the developmental task of each stage is not mastered during that critical period, the results will ultimately affect sexual adjustment in marriage. This is important for us to understand. This is why sex education for our kids starts at birth and needs to be built upon throughout adolescence and into adulthood. What we learn about sex and how we manage our sexuality affects us in

---

[34] Penner, C. & Penner, J. (2003). *The Gift of Sex: A Guide to Sexual Fulfillment.* Nashville, TN: W Publishing Group.

CHAPTER 2: EDUCATE YOURSELF

relationship. Not just going into marriage, but throughout our entire life.

I remember when my son was around 5 years old and I was putting him to bed one night. He was wearing his Buzz Lightyear pajamas and he asked me this question: "Dad, how come my penis gets hard?" Now, I thought to myself, "I couldn't have asked my dad this question when I was 16, let alone five years old." My son knew what his genitals were called and felt safe to ask me this question. I was able to say to him, "This is how God made you." I wanted his first question about his sexuality to be positive and connected to his Creator. I also told him, "This happens to all men and happens to me too." I was still cool when he was five. And then I said, "When you wake up in the morning, it just means you have to go pee." He said, "Alright Dad," and moved on to talking about the *Toy Story* movie.[35] Afterwards, I came downstairs and said to my wife, "I just had an amazing conversation with our son."

This conversation met my son right where he was at. It didn't answer all of the questions, but it was a piece of the puzzle. Of course, the conversation with our 5-year-old will look different than the conversation we have with our 12-year-old, but having the conversation is the important part. Family is the right place to be open about and ready for these kinds of conversations.

In our homes growing up, some of us may have had a negative experience if shame was involved in the situation. If we asked a question or were curious about something and were shamed for it—our question or curiosity was met with scolding or a shaming message—we could automatically think, *This is not*

---

[35] Arnold, B. (Producer), & Lasseter, J. (Director). (1995) *Toy Story* [Motion Picture]. United States: Pixar Animation Studios.

a safe place. A parent's reaction tells the child a lot about how to navigate their environment. And unfortunately, shame can stay with us for a very long time.

Other examples of negative interactions happen when:

- parents are silent on this subject, thinking that saying nothing is the best approach.
- kids are left to discover and stumble down this pathway blindly.
- parents overexpose their kids to sexually explicit material at an early age, directly or indirectly—television, the Internet, or video games.
- young children have an iPhone with Internet access and no supervision.
- family secrets are discovered, not disclosed, like an affair or divorce.

All of these examples can leave a child without the framework to deal with their own questions about sexuality.

We will talk about various ways and at what ages to educate our children regarding safety and boundaries throughout this book. There are many resources now available to educate ourselves and our kids and keep them safe. There are many experienced voices and opportunities for education in the home and in the classroom for kids and parents in this area—resources we can use and go through with our kids at all stages of their development.

I have included a list of recommended resources in the appendix. One resource I highly recommend is the *Learning About Sex Series*, which has books for girls and boys of different age

CHAPTER 2: EDUCATE YOURSELF

groups.[36] There are several other children's books I have read and would recommend. *It's Not the Stork*, by Robie Harris, does a great job of explaining anatomy and the process of puberty, conception, and childbirth, though it is not written from a faith-based perspective.[37] As parents, not every book will have our same values, but could create an excellent opportunity to talk about values: explain where our values come from and why they may be different from others. Being able to teach respect for others, even though their values may be different than ours, is part of training our children.

Many parents find it difficult to say anything to their kids about sexuality. The old-school way of doing things was to have one talk with your pre-teen child, hand them a book, and say, "Read this and let me know if you have any questions," hoping they wouldn't have any questions. When I was 12 years old, my mom gave me a book from a grocery story. It took me about two minutes to read it—because it only had five pictures—and I was done. I didn't actually read it.

Even when my wife and I were raising our children, we pushed the ball forward a bit, but still did not have the full picture of how to educate our kids from birth to adulthood. This is one of the advantages of having the Internet: there is an abundance of information available to us. This information is also available to our kids and not all of it is correct or helpful, which is why it's so important that we are their first educators.

---

[36] Learning About Sex Book Series. Concordia Publishing House. Retrieved from https://www.cph.org/c-2910-learning-about-sex.aspx.

[37] Harris, R. (2008). *It's Not the Stork!: A Book About Girls, Boys, Babies, Bodies, Families and Friends*. Somerville, MA: Candlewick Press.

Whatever our own experience was, most of us would agree that historically the topic of sex and healthy sexuality has been a difficult subject for parents to know how to communicate. The good news is, as families, we walk through all of these stages with our kids and will have ongoing opportunities to influence them, educate ourselves and them, and even make and correct our mistakes. We are given the privilege of walking alongside our kids. We don't need to know everything and we don't need to dispense all of the information at once.

At times, we will also have the opportunity to grow along with them. We first have to understand and own it for ourselves and then begin to let it come out in conversation. As we continue to work on our own personal health and add to our own education and understanding, we will be better equipped to take this journey with our kids. Hopefully, we will be able to go beyond what many of our parents gave us.

FAITH COMMUNITIES

Catholic or Protestant, Atheist, Amish or Jewish—our faith traditions play a role in how we view and communicate about our sexuality. We are part of communities that are a subculture of the culture we live in, at large, and we are deeply influenced by them. If we are taught that we are made in the image of God, that God is relational, and that our sexuality was created by God, we will have a better starting point. If we are taught that all sexual urges and feelings as a young person moving toward puberty are "lust and evil," then our teenage years will be filled with tremendous tension. This will impact our adult lives, whether we are trying to live as a single or married adult.

CHAPTER 2: EDUCATE YOURSELF

Faith communities sometimes portray sexuality as a negative aspect of the human experience. Holiness can be seen as a list of dos and don'ts that keep us in God's favor and from His wrath. I sometimes say, "Healthy is the new holy." This may sound sacrilegious to some, but what I'm saying is that we have represented holiness to mean one thing: morally squeaky clean. I believe holiness is about being healthy individuals and communities of faith. This is so much more than following a list of rules. It is about true transformation—living spirituality. It always goes back to being made in the image of God and simply reflecting the other-centered, self-giving love of the Trinity. This is not negative. This is very positive.

Unfortunately, some faith communities have been a source of real damage in the area of sexuality. With sexual abuse at the hands of religious leaders—clergy, priests, and those in spiritual authority within Catholic, Protestant, and other religious groups—it's no wonder so many people have left the faith because of the damage created in the name of God. My heart aches for the victims who have suffered in this way and for the many who have lived in silence for years, if not decades.

I am grateful for organizations and individuals who are defending the abused and taking steps to bring healing to the pain that was caused. One of my friends in North Idaho is a lawyer who feels his life calling is to represent victims of religious abuse in America and change church policy for the protection of children in these environments. His firm has won many cases, helping to turn the tide of suffering and abuse that has happened at the hand of faith institutions. It breaks my heart that faith communities haven't always been the healthiest places for people in the area of sexuality. This must change. We have to reclaim what is good and healthy about our human sexuality and seek to bring restoration to those who have been wounded. I believe the day will come when the Church is seen as a place of contributing to health and wholeness in all areas of life, especially with our sexuality.

Our current faith communities can also send the message that if we have made mistakes in the area of sexuality, we are damaged goods. Although the natural consequence of negative choices can certainly be damaging, lowering shame is a big part of the path to healing. Again, the shame message is about our human worth, not about our actions. **IF WE TEACH SEXUAL RESPONSIBILITY WITH A NON SHAME-BASED APPROACH, THIS CAN HELP MINIMIZE THE CONFUSION OUR SEXUAL BEHAVIORS BRING.**

There can also be a strong emphasis on purity from faith communities, without the necessary training prior to marriage. It's sometimes easier to just tell our children what not to do, than to get in the arena with them and discuss it. Sometimes the only message we get about sexuality prior to marriage is negative: "All sexual feelings are lust" or "Arousal is bad." We don't view sexual intercourse as good, or recognize that it was created for and best expressed in a committed, monogamous relationship of marriage. **In reality, sex is good, sex is from God, God is sexual, and we are made in His image.** In some faith communities these things were seen as almost evil and the topic is avoided.

Our sexuality comes from God. I see this as *we are made in God's image*.[38] God is sexual. This may be a difficult thought to wrestle with or something you haven't considered. The ability to create, to bond, and to feel deep pleasure comes from God. All

---

[38] Genesis 1:27

CHAPTER 2: EDUCATE YOURSELF

of the parts and functions of our body are made by God. Both male and female are made in God's image. Our sex, male and female, and the bonding of sexual intercourse were created to reflect this love. When they are lived out and shared in a healthy way, love and the best interest of others' are always at the center.

There is a passage of Scripture that clearly speaks about this, in my opinion, in the Message version by Eugene Peterson.[39] It uses great language to communicate the author's heart in modern day language.

> THERE'S MORE TO SEX THAN MERE SKIN ON SKIN. SEX IS AS MUCH SPIRITUAL MYSTERY AS PHYSICAL FACT. AS WRITTEN IN SCRIPTURE, "THE TWO BECOME ONE." SINCE WE WANT TO BECOME SPIRITUALLY ONE WITH THE MASTER, WE MUST NOT PURSUE THE KIND OF SEX THAT AVOIDS COMMITMENT AND INTIMACY, LEAVING US MORE LONELY THAN EVER—THE KIND OF SEX THAT CAN NEVER "BECOME ONE." THERE IS A SENSE IN WHICH SEXUAL SINS ARE DIFFERENT FROM ALL OTHERS. IN SEXUAL SIN WE VIOLATE THE SACREDNESS OF OUR OWN BODIES, THESE BODIES THAT WERE MADE FOR GOD-GIVEN AND GOD-MODELED LOVE, FOR "BECOMING ONE" WITH ANOTHER. OR DIDN'T YOU REALIZE THAT YOUR BODY IS A SACRED PLACE, THE PLACE OF THE HOLY SPIRIT? DON'T YOU SEE THAT YOU CAN'T LIVE HOWEVER YOU PLEASE, SQUANDERING WHAT GOD PAID SUCH A HIGH PRICE FOR? THE PHYSICAL PART OF YOU IS NOT SOME PIECE OF PROPERTY BELONGING TO THE SPIRITUAL PART OF YOU. GOD OWNS THE WHOLE WORKS. SO LET PEOPLE SEE GOD IN AND THROUGH YOUR BODY.

---

[39] 1 Corinthians 6:16-7:4 MSG

NOW, GETTING DOWN TO THE QUESTIONS YOU ASKED IN YOUR LETTER TO ME. FIRST, IS IT A GOOD THING TO HAVE SEXUAL RELATIONS? CERTAINLY—BUT ONLY WITHIN A CERTAIN CONTEXT. IT'S GOOD FOR A MAN TO HAVE A WIFE, AND FOR A WOMAN TO HAVE A HUSBAND. SEXUAL DRIVES ARE STRONG, BUT MARRIAGE IS STRONG ENOUGH TO CONTAIN THEM AND PROVIDE FOR A BALANCED AND FULFILLING SEXUAL LIFE IN A WORLD OF SEXUAL DISORDER. THE MARRIAGE BED MUST BE A PLACE OF MUTUALITY—THE HUSBAND SEEKING TO SATISFY HIS WIFE, THE WIFE SEEKING TO SATISFY HER HUSBAND. MARRIAGE IS NOT A PLACE TO "STAND UP FOR YOUR RIGHTS." MARRIAGE IS A DECISION TO SERVE THE OTHER, WHETHER IN BED OR OUT.

We want to teach our kids that purity isn't something we just do before we get married. It's a way of managing our life, whether married or single. Holiness and purity could be thought of as synonyms, both describing healthy relationship with ourselves and others. Purity (healthy relationships) is a way of life.

For some of us it is hard to believe that Jesus—who claimed to be God, yet claimed to be fully man—was human just like every other man. He would have faced attraction, sexual feelings, and arousal, yet He would have managed all of this in loving ways toward Himself and others. Think about this for a minute. Go back and read this paragraph again. Do you believe this is true? It's usually easier to skip over this part of Jesus.

I have come to believe that God has such a high and valued view of humanity that He became one of us, in all ways, yet without sin.[40]

---

[40] Author Paul Young shared this in a service I attended.

CHAPTER 2: EDUCATE YOURSELF

More and more faith communities are embracing sexuality and humanity from a positive perspective. There are many faith-based ministries and counseling centers that have provided a positive voice to parents and kids. Many local churches are talking about recovery and healthy sexuality.

Where there has been open dialogue about sexuality, it has created healthier environments where sexuality is not seen as a taboo subject. There is a desire to be vulnerable and show up as who we really are. This is messy but so freeing. This will send a redeeming message to our kids. As faith communities come together to talk about grief, trauma, addiction, and share stories, this lends itself to deeper community and connection, which is what we need most.

We are made for intimate relationships and faith communities are a huge part of this potential—this should, in fact, be their very focus. Together, as we participate in a faith community through teaching environments, small groups, recovery groups, serving our community and extended families, and more, we actually become part of this hope.

We have the opportunity to be a strong voice as families and faith communities, and affect culture rather than the other way around.

Because of the huge impact culture is having on our children today, I want to spend a considerable amount of time focusing on the education and resources we need to help us raise awareness and hopefully turn the tide of healthy sexuality in our culture. We have to start somewhere to make a dent in this area and create positive change. This first starts with understanding what is happening. As parents and grandparents, many of us grew up in a different era. For young parents, you know that culture continues to change at a rapid rate, purposely targeting our kids.

CULTURE

PORNOGRAPHY AND A HYPERSEXUALIZED CULTURE

My wife and I had the privilege of attending a conference at Gonzaga University in Spokane, Washington. The title of the conference was "Pornography: The New Drug." It was an impactful event, so I want to highlight a few things I learned. A couple key things stood out to me. This was a partnership of several organizations and individuals, from both faith and non-faith backgrounds, coming together to shine a light on the public health crisis of pornography and a hypersexualized pop culture that is targeting our kids in a multitude of ways. I was impressed by the fact that people of all backgrounds saw the importance of linking arms around a shared desire to have a culture of respect and to fight against the billion dollar pornography industry. Surely the Divine smiles at this.

The second thing that impressed me was the enormity of what is going on behind the scenes, that we are sometimes oblivious to, and the speed at which it is growing. Most of us want to be informed parents, but we only know the tip of the iceberg when it comes to understanding what the potential dangers are for our kids. One of the speakers at the conference was Dr. Gail Dines, president of Culture Reframed, and writer of a book called *Pornland: How Porn Has Hijacked Our Sexuality*.[41] She has been described as "the world's leading anti-pornography campaigner"[42] and has studied the effects of porn for nearly 30

---

[41] Dines, G. (2010). *Pornland: How Porn Has Hijacked Our Sexuality.* Boston, MA: Beacon Press.

[42] Bindel, J. (2010). The Truth About the Porn Industry. *The Guardian.* Retrieved from https://www.theguardian.com/lifeandstyle/2010/jul/02/gail-dines-pornography.

CHAPTER 2: EDUCATE YOURSELF

years. She is a straight shooter who is influencing culture in a variety of ways and spoke directly about many of the growing dangers for our kids. Mainstream porn, which comes up within seconds of a Google search, is hardcore porn—it represents "sexual cruelty and brutality, where women are subject to body-punishing sex and called vile names."[43]

This is a fascinating social experiment. Dines went on to explain that we have never before raised a generation of boys on hardcore porn. "The consequences for our culture are that boys grow to be men who view women as disposable objects and themselves as predators and women who see their roles as victims, as dictated by the porn/entertainment industry."[44] Dines shared about the effects of a "pornified culture," where we not only have a portion of young men and more and more young women being exposed and often times addicted to pornography, but we also have the majority of the rest of our adolescents being inundated by the culture, exploring and being greatly affected by the desire to "fit in."

Young women, in an attempt to not be "invisible," are playing into what our culture and the pornography industry characterizes as "normal." Therefore, they do what they believe will get them noticed or accepted. A mom who wants her daughter to dress modestly and a daughter who wants to fit in are both doing what they believe they need to do. This knowledge can help parents to be more understanding when there is a struggle. Many more young women than ever are also being pulled into an addiction to pornography itself.

---

[43] Oliva, A. (2019). Pornography: The New Drug. Catholic Medical Association. Spokane, WA: Gonzaga University. Retrieved from https://www.gonzaga.edu/news-events/stories/2019/2/15/porn-conference-2019.

[44] Ibid.

All of us see our young girls trying to fit in, whether it is their dress, attitudes and language, body image issues, or a chosen pose for a selfie. We shouldn't be surprised or be angry with them. If there is anyone to be angry at, it's the pornography industry that is targeting them.[45]

Many young men and women are getting their understanding and preferences for sexual experiences from more and more violent portrayals of what it means to be sexual. This is setting up their sexual understanding and expectations, from the beginning, to be unrealistic—often disconnected or desensitized to degrading or violent acts.[46] This is a part of shaping what an adolescent finds sexually arousing.

Each of us has an arousal template that is influenced early on and directs what our preferences are sexually—what we will find sexually stimulating or arousing. This generally comes from our early experiences. Dr. Patrick Carnes refers to this as, "The total constellation of thoughts, images, behaviors, sounds, smells, sights, fantasies, and objects that arouse us sexually. This constellation encompasses vast categories of stimuli that come from our early experiences with family, friends, religious affiliations, media, and teachers."[47]

---

[45] Gale Dines, (2019). Catholic Medical Association: Conference on Pornography: The New Drug. Gonzaga University. YouTube.

[46] Carnes, P. (2009). *Facing the Shadow: Starting Sexual and Relationship Recovery* (2nd ed.). Carefree, AZ: Gentle Path Press.

[47] Carnes, P. (2015). *Facing the Shadow: Starting Sexual and Relationship Recovery* (3rd ed.). Carefree, AZ: Gentle Path Press.

CHAPTER 2: EDUCATE YOURSELF

Culturally there is a lot of sexual experimentation on college campuses.[48] Violence and higher-risk activities are pursued and become the norm. Dating has been replaced with sexual hookups. This behavior begins in a student's teen years with the rise of sexting and sharing nude photos. There's a lot of pressure on our kids and young adults in the area of sexuality, so they need to be able to talk about it and have healthy conversation in churches, schools, and especially their homes.

Conversation is happening about the rise of young men with ED (erectile dysfunction).[49] Pornography sets up people to be in full control of these hypersexualized experiences (sometimes called supranormal or exaggerated stimulus). This can make it very difficult for young men to have real-life connections with others. Real relationships are messy and complicated. When young men begin to let go of the habitual behavior, their desire for real experiences increases.

It is hard to keep up with the changes in exposure to our kids. The pornography industry is constantly changing.[50] It is no longer a "mom and pop" type of industry, selling magazines at the corner drug store. With technology our young people have instant access to images and harmful messages they are not ready to process. The company MindGeek, who now owns approximately 80 percent of the market on pornography, is

---

[48] Jenson, K. (2019). *10 Reasons Colleges are Producing Rapists Like Brock Turner.* Protect Young Minds. Retrieved from https://www.protectyoungminds.org/2016/06/09/10-reasons-colleges-producing-rapists/

[49] Fight The New Drug, (2018). *PIED 101: The Science Behind Porn-Induced Erectile Dysfunction.* Retrieved from https://fightthenewdrug.org/science-behind-porn-induced-erectile-dysfunction/.

[50] Gale Dines, (2019). Catholic Medical Association: Conference on Pornography: The New Drug. Gonzaga University. YouTube.

putting their financial and political power toward marketing to our kids.[51] MindGeek is "the largest adult entertainment operator globally," according to the Porn Industry Press.[52] They own PornHub, which is the largest pornographic distributor. **WITH THE SPEED IN WHICH TECHNOLOGY CHANGES, IT IS HARD TO KEEP UP FOR OURSELVES, LET ALONE KNOW WHAT OUR KIDS ARE FACING.** This may seem overwhelming.

I'm giving you this information not to overwhelm you but to make you aware of how our culture is working hard for the attention of our kids and, in many ways, developing strategies to entrap them. The pornography industry is working closely with technology industries, such as cell phone companies, to target our kids.

Just know that you do not need to necessarily be a technology wizard and keep up on everything, but it is helpful to know what resources are available to help keep your family informed and safe. There are some organizations with websites and other resources that are dedicated to specifically keeping up on what is changing in technology, how it is targeting our kids, and what we can do about it. A couple of good online resources are Common Sense Media and NetSmartz.[53, 54]

Pornography used to be something we could perhaps ignore or think it is not going to affect us or our family. We could think, *We're a family with strong values and faith. This won't affect us.*

While not all kids and teenagers will develop an addiction to pornography, their dress and selfies, sexting, media, music,

---

[51] Bindel, J. (2010). The Truth About the Porn Industry. *The Guardian.* Retrieved from https://www.theguardian.com/lifeandstyle/2010/jul/02/gail-dines-pornography.

[52] Ibid.

[53] Common Sense Media: www.commonsensemedia.org/.

[54] NetSmartz: www.netsmartz.org/Training.

CHAPTER 2: EDUCATE YOURSELF

language, and attitudes are deeply affected by culture, those around them, and a desire to fit in.

This is not an "outside the Church" problem. This affects kids in our churches, youth groups, and in our homes possibly just as much. Often, our kids who are making many good moral choices become trapped by cultural influences and may even deal with a secret struggle or addiction. This is why establishing open communication is so important.

There will always be a small portion of young people who are not as affected in this area as others, but all are affected—in a multitude of big and small ways. Even kids who were raised with a strong moral conviction can be pulled into pornography and sexual behavior that doesn't reflect their personal or family's values. This happens all the time, so the point is to not assume anything, but know that you can be a big part of training about healthy sexuality.

We may be tempted to put our heads in the sand until we have to face it, or wish we could lock our kids in a room until they grow up (that's an understandable reaction to wanting to protect our children), but neither of these ideas are actually helpful. The most helpful thing we can do is to open up conversation. Communication from the parents and family and concerned adults is our hope against this huge problem in our culture. Culture is speaking loudly to our kids. We must be as well.

When we are inundated with this over a period of time, we become desensitized to the dangers of it and can lose the sacredness of the gift of our sexuality. Add to this a young child's inability to process what they see, and we have the perfect storm. With more and more elementary students having iPhones and greater access to all types of technology—sometimes with little to no filters or protection—parents need to be even more proactive.

We may not even realize how easy it is to get around security software and filters. Exposure to sexual content is almost certain.

Our culture is beginning to see the negative impact on our youth and parental blocking software, such as CovenantEyes, is becoming more valuable and more effective.[55] These can never replace a safe relationship and communication, but they provide positive support to families.

Sometimes, our kids' peers are doing a lot of the educating and their information comes from where? Each other, the Internet, television, media, older siblings, or family members who may or may not have the same values as we do or may just not have the correct information.

All the messages about human sexuality from culture give us a great opportunity to observe this with our kids. We can help them see what is good and right about these messages and discuss with them the messages that are destructive. **BEING SURROUNDED BY HEALTHY PEOPLE AND COMMUNITIES GIVES OUR KIDS A CHANCE TO SEE WHAT IS POSITIVE ABOUT THEIR CULTURE.**

Historically, there are times when the pendulum swings, and we, as a culture, see the devastation our views create and begin to do something. The rise of sexual brokenness, greater understanding of brain science, and the consequences of a disconnected culture may work together, contributing to a greater awareness and allow the pendulum to swing back with positive results. Awareness may just wake up our society and create a change in direction. This appears to be the case with many organizations inside and outside of the United States. Raising awareness helps parents understand what's going on so they can help their kids navigate through it. There is a deep

---

[55] CovenantEyes Screen Accountability. Retrieved from www.covenanteyes.com.

CHAPTER 2: EDUCATE YOURSELF

thread of truth that runs through our world that points us back to God's love.

We also must link arms with those of all faith and non faith backgrounds. One of the porn industry's efforts is to undermine anyone who stands against this epidemic by making it a "religious" issue, saying people shouldn't be denied this right.[56] This is why communities of professionals and organizations are declaring that pornography addiction is not a moral issue but a "public health crisis." Once upon a time, smoking tobacco was not regulated. Attempts to regulate smoking were considered a religious idea.

Many people, both inside and outside of faith traditions, are bringing attention and a voice to the fact that early exposure to pornography changes the brain, creates trauma for our children, and contributes to the increasing violence and degrading of women and men.[57]

This doesn't mean we set aside our different values between faiths and even between our cultures and families; but there is so much good that comes from us linking arms in the bigger truths we agree upon and want to teach our children. It is hopeful that we have a society who sees the danger of disconnection and a lack of intimacy.

---

[56] Oliva, A. (2019). Pornography: The New Drug. Catholic Medical Association. Spokane, WA: Gonzaga University. Retrieved from https://www.gonzaga.edu/news-events/stories/2019/2/15/porn-conference-2019.

[57] Ibid.

PUBLIC SEX EDUCATION

One area of tension and different points of view still exists in the sex education being taught in our schools.[58] This concern comes from the inconsistency in mandated sex education in our country. In the United States, just under half the states have mandated sex education, with varying requirements. Within each state, what is taught may vary by different schools and districts.

The concern stems from teaching our kids safe sex instead of abstinence, as well as teaching on heterosexual and homosexual relationships. The different states do not always agree. The negative effects of these inconsistencies is that the United States has continued to have a higher rate of unplanned pregnancies and STDs. Oral sex is common among teenagers, even within the church. So, without the appropriate sex education and greater understanding of sexual behaviors, this makes our kids vulnerable to STDs and other choices with negative consequences.

The emotional impact around issues with sexting and other forms of sexual promiscuity among teens is another factor. Many young people who have not been educated and thought through the consequences find themselves involved in sexual experiences that they did not intend. If we don't give our children knowledge and understanding about how to make good choices around their sexual behaviors, they are often blindly navigating this part of their lives.

The definition of a comprehensive sex education program "includes age-appropriate, medically accurate information on a broad set of topics related to sexuality including human

---

[58] National Conference of State Legislatures (2019). State Policies on Sex Education in Schools. Retrieved from http://www.ncsl.org/research/health/state-policies-on-sex-education-in-schools.aspx.

development, relationships, decision-making, abstinence, contraception, and disease prevention."[59]

Along with this comprehensive approach, they teach contraception use and help students make choices around when they will say Yes or No to sexual experiences and why they should make these choices. This can be uncomfortable for parents who want an abstinence-only message taught to their children.

Some countries are attempting to take a holistic view of teaching sexuality to kids. Europeans, particularly the Dutch, have paved the way for early education on sexuality.[60] They begin educating their children on anatomy, consent, and respect for themselves and others in kindergarten. This is a yearly requirement within their education curriculum. They also teach on the dangers of disconnection and the harm of pornography in developing healthy relationship.

The positive effect of this approach is that they are starting early and, every year, teaching kids about their sexuality in the classroom throughout their school years. Human sexuality is more than just the act of sex. The kids are more informed, comfortable talking about it, have a better understanding of their bodies and how sexuality works, and it's all happening in a safe environment. They are learning about moral choices. They are invited to ask questions and given medically accurate information. The difficulty can be when the teacher's viewpoint or the curriculum does not match the values of the parent.

---

[59] Harley, C. (2019). *Sex ed for social change.* Sexuality Information and Education Council of the United States. Retrieved from https://siecus.org/sex-ed-is-a-vehicle-for-social-change/.

[60] Melker, S. (2015). *The case for starting sex education in kindergarten.* PBS News Hour. Retrieved from https://www.pbs.org/newshour/health/spring-fever.

However, for an involved parent, they're able to talk with their kids about their values and why their perspective is different.

This is a dilemma for those of us who believe God designed us to express sexuality within marriage. With our kids, we don't intend to send the message that it's okay to have sex when they "believe" they're ready, to give them birth control, and to endorse this behavior. However, if we don't do our part as parents—share our values and talk openly about our kid's sexual choices—it can backfire. **WITHOUT UNDERSTANDING, IT IS HARD FOR OUR KIDS TO STAND AGAINST THE BOMBARDMENT OF CULTURE, AND THE INTENSE SEXUAL FEELINGS THAT COME WITH GROWING INTO ADULTHOOD, AND BE ABLE TO MAKE HEALTHY CHOICES.**

As parents, we also have the important assignment of continuing to love and accept our children, and others around us, when they think differently than us. John 13:35 says, "By this everyone will know that you are my disciples, if you love one another." Too often, we are known as Jesus' disciples by our stance on certain topics or our belief systems, rather than our love for others.

We may choose to homeschool or put our kids in a private school, but they will still be exposed to our culture. Therefore, the very best defense is a good offense, so to speak, when it comes to training our children in the area of sexuality.

If parents aren't taking on this role, and kids aren't getting sex education in faith communities or the classroom, there will be a huge void in our culture of healthy information getting to our kids. They are going to Google it, view it, and share it with each other.

Finding out what your school district is teaching (or not teaching) regarding sexuality is an important place to start. Then,

CHAPTER 2: EDUCATE YOURSELF

being able to come alongside your children to answer questions and share why you have chosen your set of beliefs and values is the best way to help them.

It should be very apparent why we must take on the responsibility to be the primary sex educators of our children. We can and should cooperate with others to convey positive messages to our kids, but it is us, as parents, who will be able to talk through the specific values that we want to pass on.

In our current digital age, we have access to good information, the opportunity to be more informed, and to share this knowledge with others. We, as parents, have the ability to look at what is and isn't working and to use this knowledge for the benefit of our kids. If we are aware of what is offered and we stay involved, culture can contribute to many good learning opportunities.

In my community, when my kids were in public elementary school, getting ready to transition to middle school, the school had a parent-student meeting for moms and daughters and one for dads and sons. During these meetings, they led conversations about puberty, the changes happening to our bodies during adolescence, and they created an opportunity for parents and kids to discuss this issue together. I appreciate our school district for hosting this event and helping parents cultivate conversation with their kids about sexuality.

I was recently invited to visit this school (almost 15 years later) to share with the young boys and their fathers about sexual health. I'm continuing to help our school district with their education program and promoting healthy sexuality.

From one parent to another, I want to challenge you. How can we help culture rather than fight culture? How can we be part of the answer, not part of the problem? Clearly, part of the answer comes from not being silent. I'm glad I didn't pull away from culture in this matter, but rather engaged in culture to be an influence on it. I'm still engaged in culture, not only for the sake of my own kids but of others.

Our children are going to face sexual pressures. Here's how we can help:

- Start training our kids when they're young.
- Educate ourselves so we can educate our kids.
- Explain the reasons why we choose our values.

If it seems like I've brought a lot of attention to our culture, it's because I want you to clearly see that culture is and will continue to educate our kids if we don't. We must not be silent on this topic!

CHAPTER 2

TRY THIS!

CHOOSE ONE AREA TO GAIN MORE EDUCATION IN AND TRY IT THIS WEEK: BUY A BOOK, WATCH A YOUTUBE VIDEO ON PARENTING, OR LISTEN TO A PODCAST. CHECK OUT A RESOURCE FROM THE APPENDIX.

OR

JOIN OR START A GROUP TO CONNECT AND GROW WITH OTHER PARENTS IN YOUR COMMUNITY.

QUESTIONS

1 | Growing up, who was your primary educator about sexuality: family, faith tradition, or culture? Was your experience more positive or negative?

2 | How did your family of origin educate you on sex?

3 | How did the information on culture impact you? In what ways could you begin to think about influencing culture?

4 | What are you doing to make yourself the primary educator of your children? What is one way you would like to improve?

5 | Read the passage from 1 Corinthians on page 39. What stands out most in this text?

CHAPTER 3

PRACTICE COMMUNICATION

Penis, testicles, erection, vagina, wet dreams, masturbation, menstrual cycle, ejaculation, intercourse, just to name a few words surrounding our sexuality. How's this for the start to chapter 3? These words and concepts can be difficult for many of us to talk about, especially if we're not used to using sexual words or language.

Many of us grew up not talking about sexuality in a healthy way or sometimes not talking about it at all, so this can be a challenge. Even hearing language like this as adults makes us feel uncomfortable. Sometimes we have only heard these words in a degrading way.

If we're going to help our kids in the area of sexuality, we first need to get comfortable with this language and understanding it for ourselves. We don't have the luxury of avoiding the subject in the world in which we live—expecting our kids will be okay and able to figure it out without negative consequences. In many ways, I am grateful that an openness in culture is forcing us to face this subject head on. The negative consequences of not talking about it have always been there, but we didn't always see it as clearly. We want to learn how to articulate our thoughts and beliefs in the area of sexuality, starting with the fact that it is good.

Some couples have sex regularly but never actually talk to each other about it: what brings them pleasure, what may be difficult or challenging, or addressing their own body parts. The more comfortable couples are talking about their shared sexuality, thoughts, and feelings—and the more comfortable an individual is with their own sexuality—the easier it will be to articulate what kids need to know in their sexual development. This will prepare us, as parents, to share with our kids.

A great way to start developing our sexual language is by reading a resource or book out loud as an individual or couple and discussing the ideas with your spouse or a trusted friend or family member. This could be a book (or video) about your own sexuality or sex in marriage or about information on sharing sexuality with your kids. This could also include using this book—the one you're reading right now—a chapter at a time, reading it out loud and discussing the questions.

I also recommend getting some books written for children and reading them out loud to yourself and to each other first, before reading them with your child. When you do this, it creates an openness and familiarity in hearing and using these words. Then, when the time comes, you're more easily able to share them with your child.

When we begin to share these concepts with our children, it doesn't need to be communicated just fathers with sons or mothers with daughters. **CREATING OPEN FAMILY CONVERSATIONS, WHERE FAMILY MEMBERS KNOW IT'S ALWAYS SAFE TO TALK ABOUT SEX AND ASK QUESTIONS, CAN FOSTER A GREAT LEARNING ENVIRONMENT.** Parents can also have specific conversations together with one child or may determine that some things are better expressed one on one.

CHAPTER 3: PRACTICE COMMUNICATION

This whole process can be something new for many people. It pushes us out of our comfort zone. It causes us to look not only at communicating language but also our values and the lens through which we view the world.

It's important to think about and know our personal family values and why we have them. Were they given to us by our parents or someone else, or have we established them on our own? What were the spoken *and* unspoken messages we received? What do we want to pass on to our children and what is the reason behind this? Why do we hold specific values?

As we are educating ourselves and learning, we need to think about our personal value system and own these values. As parents, we need to decide what and how to share our values with our kids.

Many of us grew up with a way of thinking, a certain paradigm that someone handed us, as the absolute truth; only later to realize that we were misguided or needed a different way of seeing the world—we needed a different lens to look through. Trying on a different lens helps us to see in a new way and determine if that lens is a better fit—something we want to hold on to.

HEALTHY VS. UNHEALTHY

In the conservative Christian paradigm I grew up in, it was a pretty black and white, right or wrong world. There were a lot of rules. Everything seemed to be a sin and the lines were quite blurry. I now joke about it this way: "Playing cards led to movies, movies led to dancing, dancing led to sex, and sex led to the worst sin of all, bowling."

We thought holiness was about moral perfection instead of being relationally healthy. Everything in my Church culture was either Christian or secular, divided into these two categories—Christian friends or non-Christian friends, Christian music or non-Christian music. By the way, *Happy Birthday* is not a Christian song.

In my opinion, this philosophy breaks down quickly. We don't have Christian tacos and non-Christian tacos. We don't say, "Are you having Christian sex or non-Christian sex?" We don't actually talk this way.

A better context to talk about all of life is, "What's healthy and what's unhealthy?" In the right context things can be healthy, but if misused or mismanaged, they can become unhealthy. I think healthy is a better way to think about the Divine. The Divine is healthy in a relational context—other centered and self-giving. Here's a great way to test my theory: every time you see the word holy substitute the word healthy. As I've mentioned before, "Healthy is the new holy." Why? Because being holy is about right relationship—in relation to others and the world we live in.

I like this framework even when we talk about sexuality. There's a healthy way to understand and manage our sexuality and there's an unhealthy way.

MANAGEMENT VS. MISMANAGEMENT

We manage our time. We manage our money. We manage our emotions. These aren't right or wrong things, good or bad. I think our sexuality is something else that we're given to manage—something of which to be stewards. When I say sexuality, I'm including the areas of our feelings, thoughts, emotions, and behaviors. Having sexual feelings and arousal are normal. This happens to everyone and isn't always something we control. However, we have control over how we handle our sexual behavior. We have the responsibility for what we do

CHAPTER 3: PRACTICE COMMUNICATION

with it—to manage it in a healthy way—and when we aren't managing well, to seek help.

In my early years of working with high school students, we would break the group up, guys and girls, and have conversations about sexuality and our faith. I would say to the 13-18-year-olds, "Guys, when you have an erection, I want you to stop and look up to God and say, "Thank you for this ability." They would look at me as if I were crazy and probably wondered if the leaders of the church knew I was teaching this crazy stuff. Then I would continue by telling them to say, "And God, help me to manage my sexual feelings and behaviors in a way that honors myself and others." I was trying to help them see that our sexuality is good—a gift from God—and the point was about making good decisions that are loving toward ourselves and others.

COMMON COMMUNICATION WITH OUR KIDS
NAMING

When it comes to our earliest stages of training, we want to start with anatomy words. Giving our children appropriate words helps them to be confident and comfortable in knowing how to communicate about their body. It also helps them if they need to communicate to us something they've experienced or communicate a boundary to someone else. We don't have to be militant about using anatomy words in every situation, but it's important that our kids know the correct words and that talking about it is normalized. It can be helpful to share with them that some slang words for our body parts are disrespectful, even sharing some of these words with older children, so we get the opportunity to communicate this to them.

TEACHING ABOUT BODY PARTS AT A YOUNG AGE HAS BECOME MUCH MORE COMMON IN THE CURRENT GENERATION RAISING KIDS. My wife and I were with friends recently talking about this subject and my friend shared that his granddaughter said, "Papa, I have a vagina. You have a penis." As you can imagine, like most of us would be, he was a little surprised but said, "Yep, that's correct" and moved on. This is actually very healthy. This child is gaining an understanding without shame and is just figuring out how life works. She stated this—her age-appropriate knowledge and information—in a matter of fact way and then focused her attention on something else. Her parents are helping her have context and healthy, open conversation.

A comical story happened when one of my sons was in preschool. He had a habit of peeing straight ahead, missing the toilet entirely, so my wife and I would have to help him point into the toilet. My mother-in-law took him to the restroom at church one Sunday. She was helping him in the stall, and he began to pee straight ahead, spraying both of them. Grandma quickly reached down and pushed his penis toward the toilet, so they both wouldn't get sprayed. My son began yelling, "Don't touch my penis. Don't touch my penis." If you know this son of mine, he is a very literal, black and white thinker. He was asserting the boundary he had learned from my wife and I, only it ended up being pretty embarrassing for Grandma. She came out of the bathroom, shared this with me, and said, "I don't know what the other people in the bathroom thought was happening, but I could have died a thousand deaths." She complimented how well I taught her grandson anatomy words and boundaries.

CHAPTER 3: PRACTICE COMMUNICATION

APPROPRIATE TOUCH

All along the way, we will be teaching and training our kids how to use the appropriate words, the context for these words, and appropriate touch. We teach them about appropriate touch in the context of going to the bathroom, taking a bath, at the doctor's office, or when parents are helping them take care of themselves. This type of touch is about keeping a child clean and safe.

We want to communicate to our child that they have control of their body. Here is an example of how we could say this: "If someone touches your private parts or tries to have you touch theirs, outside of what we have talked about as safe touch, you can say 'no' and talk to us (or a teacher) about it. Moms and dads are supposed to protect you; so, we want you to tell us if something makes you feel afraid or yucky in your stomach, even if it was a family member or someone we know."

Letting our children know they are safe to tell us, without being punished, is important for them to know. If we are openly talking about body parts and appropriate touch, then our children will potentially feel comfortable telling us if they feel unsafe.

There is a children's book that I recommend called, *I Said No!*, by Kimberly King.[61] It can be helpful to read with kids in their early elementary years. There are many other healthy resources for protecting our children. We need to communicate with them so they learn how to communicate for themselves about their body, protecting themselves, and setting boundaries.

My wife and I came across a great animated video out of the UK, about safety and being aware of abuse—keeping our

---

[61] King, Z. & King, K. (2010). *I Said No! A Kid-to-kid Guide to Keeping Private Part Private.* Weaverville, CA: Boulden Publishing.

private parts private.[62] I've included it on the resource list in the appendix. At first, it can actually be alarming to watch because it's talking about a very sensitive topic, but knowing how young children learn and how ideas stick with them, it really is brilliant. It's a clever way to communicate to kids about a very serious subject. It is done in a way that will, most likely, make an impact and stick with them, should they need to protect themselves in this way. It's themed with a dinosaur named Pantosaurus and the creative acrostic of PANTS stands for:

- **P**rivates are private.
- **A**lways remember your body belongs to you.
- **N**o means no.
- **T**alk about secrets that upset you.
- **S**peak up, someone can help.

This may be a great video to watch first, without your kids, so you can familiarize yourself with the content. Then, watching it with your kids could be the next step in creating healthy conversation around their safety.

CURIOSITY AND LEARNING

We all wonder how things work and this a part of life, not just in the area of sexuality. Kids wonder where babies come from. They are curious and wonder about how the opposite sex's parts are different than theirs. Our kids may be interested in their body parts and might discover that touching themselves in a particular way brings pleasure. These behaviors are all natural

---

[62] National Society for the Prevention of Cruelty to Children, (2019). Teach your child the Underwear Rule. https://www.nspcc.org.uk/preventing-abuse/keeping-children-safe/underwear-rule/.

CHAPTER 3: PRACTICE COMMUNICATION

parts of curiosity. For most kids it will not become a habit and they will naturally lose interest.[63]

If your two-year-old keeps putting his hands down his pants, it doesn't mean he's a pervert. He is just curious and needs instruction. In a calm way, you can communicate with him about when this behavior is appropriate. If you've already had this conversation and he keeps doing it, you could simply redirect his attention to something else, remind him of the previous conversation, or even ask if he needs to go to the bathroom. It may be just a temporary habit, and talking to him about it in a way that doesn't shame or overfocus on it can help. If it seems like a habit or more serious problem, you could talk to someone about it or see a counselor.

If young children show interest in or attraction to others this is also normal. Remember, they don't have the sexualized brain of an adult, so it doesn't mean the same thing to them as it does to adults. One of my sons, when he was around three years old, saw a beautiful blonde on the cover of a magazine. He turned to his mother and said, "I want her to hold me." He was a pretty affectionate child anyway, and he suddenly wasn't as interested in Mom holding him. This was more funny than alarming to my wife.

IF WE NORMALIZE SEXUAL FEELINGS AND ATTRACTION, SO THE CHILD DOESN'T THINK, *WHAT'S WRONG WITH ME?*, IT CREATES AN EASIER WAY TO HELP THEM MANAGE THEIR FEELINGS. They are less likely to feel shame because they won't automatically assume they are being lustful. If they realize that attraction is a normal part of development, they will be less likely to develop shame around their sexuality and learn to manage

---

[63] Penner, C. & Penner, J. (2003). *The Gift of Sex: A Guide to Sexual Fulfillment.* Nashville, TN: W Publishing Group.

their feelings in a healthy way. It is crucial that we normalize and validate our children's experiences even while we may give them corrective information at the same time.

How we manage our feelings helps us separate what is natural from what is lust. This leads to managing our sexuality and taking responsibility for our behaviors throughout our lifetime.

It isn't always easy to find the right way to communicate with our children. We need to take advantage of opportunities wherever we see them. Parents will sometimes share with an older child or a more outgoing child, even in front of their quieter sibling, as a way of getting a message across. **It's great to let our younger children know that this is information to share as a family and in the right environment, not necessarily to share with their friends.** When we have conversations with them and explain things to them, this builds up their confidence.

Naming body parts, communicating appropriate touch, and validating sexual curiosity are all ways we communicate and an integral part of training our younger children. The conversation will continue to advance as our kids progress in age and maturity.

EXPOSURE TO PORNOGRAPHY IN MEDIA

We talked about how our culture has been hijacked by pornography in the previous chapter and how exposure is happening at a younger age. This has a powerful affect on a child's brain and, for many of our children, it can be a pattern that lasts into adulthood. We can't afford to wait until middle school to begin the conversation regarding the dangers of pornography.

We need to have the understanding and then the words to be able to communicate this to our kids in a way that they comprehend. The book, *Good Pictures Bad Pictures*, is great to read

CHAPTER 3: PRACTICE COMMUNICATION

with young children early on, educating them on the dangers of pornography and how it affects their brain. The authors write, "We teach our kids not to run out into the streets. It is dangerous. Porn is dangerous for your brain."[64] When we encourage conversation with our grade school-aged child and share how we have seen these images and have been curious too—that this type of curiosity is normal—our kids learn that they can always talk to us about it. Also, we can talk about our own exposure to pornography and how we felt about it, using age-appropriate language, without being overly graphic.

There are some simple ways to communicate about pictures and potential dangers of devices, such as a cell phone or computer. If we have talked with our children ahead of time, then when they are exposed to something inappropriate—and the word is *when*, not *if*—they will have some context: "My dad (or mom) talked to me about this." This gives them a better chance of coming to us and talking about it when they first see something. It is not shameful or something to keep hidden. This is also helpful because most children will have a variety of conflicting internal responses when they see nudity or pornography. They may be curious, but also know this isn't right. They may be interested or drawn toward it and, at the same time, find it upsetting and disgusting.[65]

When our children are older we can talk more with them about the brain science behind it and how pornography is like

---

[64] Jenson, K. & Poyner, G. (2016). *Good Pictures Bad Pictures: Porn-proofing Today's Young Kids*. Richland, WA: Glen Cove Press.

[65] Dines, G. (2019). *COMPOSE Yourself!* Culture Reframed. Retrieved from https://www.culturereframed.org/compose-yourself/.

a drug.⁶⁶ I recently shared with some junior highers on sexuality and I described how we wear helmets on a motorcycle to protect the outside of our brain, but we also need to protect the inside of our brain.

FOR MANY YOUNG CHILDREN THE EXPOSURE, GUILT, AND SECRECY BECOMES SOMETHING THAT COULD BE A HOOK—THEY MAY CONTINUE SEEKING OUT PORNOGRAPHY WITHOUT EVEN UNDERSTANDING WHY.

If we want our children to feel comfortable talking to us about their exposure to pornography and their feelings about it, we have to lead by example with open conversation. This is our chance to help them before it becomes a pattern, bringing damage into their adulthood and possibly into their marriage. As parents, we want to be proactive with our kids early on, working on prevention not just recovery.

Without healthy input from a parent or adult, a child whose mind becomes hooked on the images of pornography is learning a skewed perspective about sex. They will easily believe that sex is a selfish act to get their own needs met, instead of seeing it as a byproduct or outcome of a healthy intimate marriage relationship. Pornography causes us to bond to images and behaviors rather than to a person.⁶⁷

We want to train our children to see the act of sex as more than just intercourse—to make the connection between sex and a committed marriage relationship. I know some parents who

---

[66] Fight The New Drug (2017). *How Porn Affects The Brain Like A Drug*. Retrieved from https://fightthenewdrug.org/how-porn-affects-the-brain-like-a-drug/.

[67] Stumbo, N. (2018). *Pornography, The Brain, and Bonding*. Focus On The Family. Retrieved from https://www.focusonthefamily.com/marriage/pornography-the-brain-and-bonding/.

CHAPTER 3: PRACTICE COMMUNICATION

talked to their son about "making love." They wanted him to know that sex is more than just the act of sexual intercourse and that making love includes how you treat one another, as well as other forms of sexual and nonsexual affection: holding hands, kissing, connecting relationally, and more. This is more than just communicating to our kids "don't." Most of the time, they don't even know what this means. Too often our teenage kids are pulled into experimenting with everything but the act of intercourse, thinking the point is just to avoid sex before marriage, STDs, or pregnancy. Without having someone communicate with them about the relational and emotional parts of their sexuality, we leave them pretty confused and uninformed.

This is where we get to reinforce that we believe sex is good and explain the best context for it—to be able to celebrate it. In the beauty of a committed relationship of marriage your mind, body, and spirit are all part of this experience.

PUBERTY

Puberty includes subjects like changes in our bodies, sexual feelings, and attraction to others.[68] For girls, this includes menstrual cycles, breast development, interest in boys, and more. For boys, this includes having erections, wet dreams, body hair and odor, and their voice changing, among other things. This is a good time to remind our kids that showering is a gift to ourselves and others, but this usually takes care of itself as they begin to discover the opposite sex.

---

[68] Dobson, J. (2005). *Preparing for Adolescence: How to Survive the Coming Years of Change.* Ventura, CA: Gospel Light.

As my boys hit this stage, I took each of them on a trip and we listened to the James Dobson series, *Preparing for Adolescence*.[69] I did this in an attempt to open up questions and conversation. My sons still tease me about this today and how they would say, "Don't bring up puberty or Dad will start talking about it again."

Years ago, a mother called me about her junior high boy. She said, "My son came home from school and said, 'Mom I've had an erection all day today and it's so annoying! I'm going to lay down in my room and hopefully it goes away!'" She continued, "Rodney, what do I do about this?" I laughed and said, "You've already done it. Your son feels safe to talk to you about the changes happening in his body." A mom in this situation could also reinforce, naturally in her communication, that during puberty there are changes that are awkward and make it difficult to navigate sometimes.

When my daughter was in middle school, my wife and I were in the backyard, and she burst out the sliding door and shouted, "Mom, I just started my period!" My wife laughed and said, "That's great, but you might not want to share it with *all* of the neighbors." My wife and I laughed because we were surprised that she shouted it, but we were so glad she felt comfortable sharing it. Helping our kids feel comfortable and open is one of the best gifts we can give them during this awkward season of life. By our verbal and nonverbal communication with them, we can create a safe environment for them to communicate what they are experiencing.

---

[69] Ibid.

CHAPTER 3: PRACTICE COMMUNICATION

RELATIONSHIPS WITH OTHERS

One of the goals in raising our kids is for them to learn to have healthy relationships with themselves and others. This can start early with training them how to make amends with others when they make mistakes in any area of their lives. Carrying this into their teenage years and adulthood trains them to take ownership for their actions and hurting others, how to empathize with others' feelings, and how to show respect. Learning this, sooner than later, can teach them the principle of recognizing and correcting mistakes.

How often have we heard about adults in our world who have gone through much of their life without ever making amends for the way they have treated others, sexually or nonsexually? If they had learned to take responsibility for their actions at a young age, they could have spared themselves and others much pain and embarrassment later in life. This is where 12-Step recovery groups have gotten it right, by owning our mistakes and making amends.

Communicating to those we've hurt in this area isn't easy. In fact, it's quite difficult. But for those of us, like myself, who have done this, it is a way of making amends, taking ownership of how our actions may have hurt others.

Early adolescence is usually the time we begin to develop more interest in others and want to figure out how to interact with them. This is a discovery period of trial and error, attraction and rejection. We want to help our kids have a strong sense of their own worth and value, mirroring this and speaking this into their lives. We're trying to help our kids set good boundaries around sexual activity, reinforcing the value of right relationships with themselves, God, and others.

This is a time of talking to our kids about sexual activity, sexual experiences, arousal, and the act of sex itself. Sex, at its best, is expressed in a committed monogamous relationship. Outside of the marriage commitment, sexual experiences can cause many challenges we want them to be aware of. We need to take the opportunity to inform our kids about the potential of unwanted pregnancy, sexually transmitted diseases, negative bonding, and emotional pain. We are trying to prepare our children for healthy, other-centered, intimate sexual bonds in their future marriage relationship.

Practicing our communication helps prepare us for crucial conversations when the time comes. It's about building our own resource bank, so we have something to draw upon when it's needed.

WE HAVE THE AWESOME RESPONSIBILITY OF BEING THE ONE WHO SHARES ABOUT LIFE AND RELATIONSHIPS WITH OUR KIDS. We have the privilege to talk to them about what it means to connect with others, show respect, have meaningful relationships, and shared experiences. Out of our story and our own experiences, we get to take our kids on this journey with us.

One of the greatest things about being a parent is sharing experiences with our kids. We love to relive positive experiences through them, such as the first time our child goes camping or rides a bike. We also have the privilege of creating deeper conversations about what life is about.

Here's what you want to remember:
- first, focus on your own personal health,
- then educate yourself, and lastly,
- keep practicing communicating this subject with others.

Then, pass this communication on to your kids. Lean into the discomfort and it will become more of a privilege than a burden. You *and* your kids will reap the benefits of this!

CHAPTER 3
TRY THIS!

IDENTIFY A PERSON (SPOUSE OR FRIEND) YOU CAN PRACTICE COMMUNICATING THESE IDEAS WITH AND SET A TIME TO PRACTICE THIS WEEK.

QUESTIONS

1 | Growing up, how was sex or sexuality communicated in your home?

2 | What part of communicating about sexuality seems to be the most difficult for you?

3 | What are your thoughts about the language used with healthy vs. unhealthy and management vs. mismanagement?

4 | What would get in the way of your willingness to have open conversations with your kids?

5 | If married, how well do you and your spouse communicate about your sexuality and sexual relationship?

CHAPTER 4

FOSTER CONNECTION

In November 1994, the movie, *The Lion King*, was released by Disney.[70] I remember watching this movie countless times with my older two kids, as they were born in '92 and '93. My kids and I would say the lines together and sing the song, "Hakuna Matata." I would roar like Mufasa and say the lines he would say to Simba in a deep voice, "Remember who you are—You are my son." I find myself laughing right now as I think of these days. When I came home from work, I would simply open the door and roar like a lion and my little boy would come running. For the next 15 minutes or so, we were on our hands and knees playing Mufasa and Simba and looking through the house for "hyenas in the pridelands." These are some great memories of connection with my son.

When my daughter, Whitney, was in elementary school, I remember playing carnival in the garage. She set up stations that her brothers and I would go through, throwing a ball to knock over pins, playing hopscotch, and visiting the refreshment station, but the one I remember the most was face painting. She would paint our faces and I still remember how much joy it brought her. It was

---

[70] Hahn, D. (Producer), Allers, R. (Director), & Minkoff, R. (Director). (1994). *The Lion King* [Motion Picture}. United States: Walt Disney Feature Animation.

so much fun that I took my shirt off and the kids painted my back and chest as well. By the time we were done, the whole family was laughing and we came in the house covered in colorful paint.

Many times, fostering connection means getting on the same level as our kids and seeing the world from their point of view. **HELPING OUR KIDS UNDERSTAND AND MANAGE THEIR SEXUALITY IS FAR MORE THAN JUST EDUCATING THEM ABOUT SEX.** It's about understanding that we are made for deep connection.

Parents may have many hobbies and activities they like that are different than their kids. However, it's important not to just focus on *our football*, *our hunting*, or *our work*, but to look at what our child's interest are and get into their world. We may sometimes be doing something that isn't that interesting to us, but it means a lot to our child.

Sometimes, connecting has a lot to do with being unselfish with our time. It could include spending time with our kids building LEGOs, playing video games, watching sports, listening to music, or playing outside. This doesn't actually have to come naturally. It's something we can grow in and become intentional about, whether or not this was modeled for us growing up.

We may not be able to connect with our kids on all levels and may naturally have more in common with some of our kids than with others. It can take some effort. It's okay if we don't connect with them in every way. We just need to be intentional about creating connection.

BONDING

From the moment of our conception we are deeply connected in the womb of another human being, our mother. We aren't born

CHAPTER 4: FOSTER CONNECTION

in isolation. We are born into a family because we were made for connection and interdependence on others. And this doesn't just mean the nuclear family, but the larger family of communities and even humanity.

The chemical oxytocin, which is often called "the love hormone" because of its contribution to bonding is connected to birthing a baby, breastfeeding, and other forms of bonding, in families and socially.[71] Moms are flooded with the hormone during the birthing process. We often recognize this as that unique nurturing bond we see in many moms and their children. At birth, a new mom's brain is flooded with it, generally causing the mother to connect deeply with her little newborn. Oxytocin also contributes to bonding in sexual activity and appears to play a role in erection and orgasm. This is why, if we are not careful, we can bond to unhealthy relationships and addictive, destructive behaviors.

When we hold, hug, and express affection to our children in healthy ways, all of this creates meaningful bonds. When our children are young, we want to continually cultivate ways to connect. As our children continue to develop, they build on the connections they made early in life. A child's ability to bond with others mirrors their ability to connect and bond with God, and understandably so, as we are created in the very image of a relational God, modeled in the Trinity.

Bonding and attachment are some of our first experiences. It is the beginning of our connection to what it means to be human and a sexual being. What a beautiful ability to be able to attach with others and with God. Our attachment with God is such an important part of training our children. It is something freely

---

[71] MacGill, M. (2017). *What is the link between love and oxytocin?* MedicalNewsToday. Retrieved from https://www.medicalnewstoday.com/articles/275795.php.

offered to us and we have the ability to tune in to it. Part of this is training our children to take on the mind of Christ in every situation, which connects us to the Spirit within us.[72] The Holy Spirit trains and guide us. The Spirit helps us recognize when something doesn't "feel" right. When we slow down and listen, the Holy Spirit prompts us about what is right and what leads to producing good things in our lives.[73]

Teaching our children to be in tune with the small voice within us helps us discern when we should say No, when we should tell someone about how we're feeling, and when we should not participate in something that is destructive. We have what my wife refers to as that inner "knower." When we "know in our knower." We all experience this. Sometimes we put different names to it, such as conscience, discernment, sixth sense, or for small children it could be explained as an "uh-oh" or a "yucky" feeling in their tummy. We need to train them to recognize this as God putting inside of us what is good and right. As our children grow, we can teach them to develop this sense of what the Spirit is saying and use it to connect with God and with what is going on inside of them. This builds and strengthens their attachment and intimacy with God.

INTIMACY

WE WERE MADE FOR INTIMATE RELATIONSHIPS, BUT SOMETIMES WE HAVE CONFUSED INTIMACY WITH SEXUALITY. A faulty message our culture can send says that if we have a deep love and connection with another person,

---

[72] Philippians 2:5-8; 1 Corinthians 2:16

[73] Galatians 5:22-23

we should sexualize it. This could be with the same sex or the opposite. This has caused a great deal of confusion in our world. I have many intimate male relationships but none of these are sexual, and I have many female intimate relationships—my mother, sister, and daughter, to name a few—but only one of these is sexual and it's with my wife. Jesus was a single male and had many intimate relationships, male and female, yet we see that none of these were sexual. **Intimacy isn't necessarily sexual.** It is also more than just sharing facts. It goes deeper to the thoughts and feelings we have. It requires taking a risk and steps toward deeper vulnerability, and authenticity—being genuine and real.

A crucial piece to intimacy is our ability to be vulnerable with others, to take off the mask, show up, and "be seen."

VULNERABILITY

Vulnerability and shame are recent buzzwords. In part, this comes from the well-respected research and writing of Brene Brown. She is a researcher whose study of shame, vulnerability, and empathy have led her to people who have a common thread of living relationally healthy lives, which she calls Wholehearted Living.[74] One of the main things that led to her writing the book, *Daring Greatly*, was experiencing the power of vulnerability. In this book, vulnerability is defined as "uncertainty, risk and emotional exposure." This can seem counterintuitive to many of us. **VULNERABILITY IS A POWERFUL WAY WE CAN CONNECT WITH OUR CHILDREN.** This can be in small,

---

[74] Brown, B. (2012). *Daring Greatly: How the Courage to Be Vulnerable Transforms the Way We Live, Love, Parent, and Lead*. London, UK: Penguin Putnam, Inc.

everyday situations, like when a mom says to her child, "I feel sad because grandpa is in the hospital." Sometimes with older kids, it could be opening up about our own dynamics with siblings, parents, or about feeling anxious about our job or finances. We sometimes think we don't want to burden our children. We don't want them to know about our struggles with work or marriage, but at an appropriate level, context, and amount, this actually helps them feel more connected to us and prepare them for when they become adults. On the flip side, an unhealthy parent can continually lay their own burdens on their child, as a way to meet the parent's needs, which would be better to do with a support person other than their children. In therapy this is sometimes referred to as enmeshment or emotional incest.[75]

Think about how you would want to share vulnerably, in just a small way, that might build some connection with your kids.

I have a friend who is dealing with the recent suicide of his 16-year-old son. As I hear his story, one of his regrets is not being more vulnerable with his son. My friend serves as a first responder at a local fire department. In the past, he struggled with the ability to process all of the trauma he witnesses through his line of work. Some years ago, he found himself struggling with depression and suicidal thoughts. He reached out to a coworker, who took him to the hospital emergency room—he had a psychological evaluation and spent some time in a behavioral health facility. He was so grateful that he was vulnerable with his friend and received help for himself, but felt hesitant to share this with his kids, uncertain of whether this would benefit them or not. In hindsight, he wishes he would have been vulnerable with his story.

---

[75] Ferree, M. (2019). Pastoral Sex Addiction Professional (PSAP) Training. International Institute for Trauma & Addiction Professionals. February.

CHAPTER 4: FOSTER CONNECTION

I can sure relate with my friend's uncertainty—when to be vulnerable and how to share my story. Fortunately, he has found grace for himself in this process and is grieving his regrets. He is using his story and vulnerability to help a number of other kids who struggle.

Sometimes we think that it's better not to share our history or struggles with our kids. Appropriate vulnerability may be what's needed to build a connection. Again, this may seem counterintuitive to many of us.

Talk with your spouse or another parenting partner about how and when to share pieces of your story.

ISOLATION

Isolation is an enemy of connection. There are two ways we can isolate ourselves: externally and internally.[76] External isolation happens when we physically separate ourselves from others and withdraw from an environment that would bring us into contact with others. Internal isolation happens when we are with others physically but we have detached ourselves internally from them. We withhold our true feelings, thoughts, and actions because we fear embarrassment, rejection, or punishment.

Sometimes the mismanagement of sexuality comes from isolation, depression, and disconnection from healthy participation in life. We need to be in tune with what's going on with our children and watching for warning signs. If we see warning signs in our kids and changes in their behavior—withdrawing from family, friends, and their environment—we need to give attention to this.

---

[76] Roberts, T. (2014). *Seven Pillars of Freedom Workbook*. Gresham, OR: Pure Desire Ministries International.

If you notice warning signs in your child's behavior, it's always okay to ask them questions about their feelings and seek professional outside help for yourself as a parent. If your child shows signs of ongoing depression or withdrawal, you may need to ask specific questions and assess the risk of suicide.[77] Resources are listed in the appendix for further help.

Conversations about how our culture is becoming more and more disconnected are more common today. We live in a lonely culture. From all outward appearances we have more ways to connect than ever, but our culture seems more distracted and more disconnected than ever. Most of us realize, we can be in a crowd and still feel extremely lonely.

DISCONNECTION LEADS TO ALL KINDS OF RELATIONSHIP PROBLEMS WITH FAMILY, FRIENDS, AND COMMUNITY. It can also lead to intimacy disorders, where people are unable to connect intimately with others, nonsexually and/or sexually.[78] Much of the work of sexual addiction and dysfunction can be traced back to a disconnection with the ability to be intimate.

In our pornified culture, the thread running through is disconnection. The pornography industry is hard at work making it look like pornography is harmless. The results of a study revealed the association between loneliness and viewing pornography was significant.[79]

Isolation also leads us to believe we are separated from God and can make us "feel" disconnected from the Divine. This is seen

---

[77] QPR (Question, Persuade, Refer) Training. Spokane, WA.

[78] Carnes, P. (1992). *Don't Call It Love: Recovery From Sexual Addiction.* New York, NY: Bantam Books.

[79] National Center on Sexual Exploitation (2018). *The Public Health Harms of Pornography.* Washington, DC: NCSE.

very clearly in Genesis 3 and the story of Adam and Eve. God was still seeking them out, but their choices and the resulting belief caused them to feel disconnected and hide. In the same way, our wrong choices blind us from seeing the truth about our connection with God—that nothing can separate us from God's love.[80]

I've experienced this and had to learn that my thoughts and feelings are not always accurate.

THOUGHTS AND FEELINGS

Sometimes it's difficult to separate our thoughts and feelings. We may not even know there is a difference. We often use the terms, "I feel this way..." when we're actually talking about what we think, not what we feel. For example, we might say, "I feel like my dad doesn't like me." This is not a feeling. This is a thought. A more accurate way to think about or express this is, "I think my dad doesn't like me, therefore, I feel sad, anxious, and rejected." These are feeling words. There is no such thing as right or wrong feelings; they are either positive or negative feelings.

Learning to separate and identify our thoughts and feelings is very important. Sometimes we generate negative feelings from our "thinking errors"—thoughts that aren't true. For example, as we look at whether our thoughts are actually true, we may replace our negative thought with some truth: "My dad does like me, he is just concerned about some of the choices I've made." If we learn this, we can become more aware and connected to ourselves. **KNOWING OURSELVES IS THE STARTING PLACE TO CONNECT AND KNOW OTHERS.** Sharing our feelings creates intimacy more than just sharing our thoughts.

---

[80] Romans 8:39

When our children are young we need to help them with these crucial steps:

1. Know that feelings aren't good or bad.
2. Understand the difference between thoughts and feelings.
3. Identify their feelings.
4. Learn how to express their feelings in healthy ways.

This can help our kids feel comfortable and free to share openly with us and other mentors in their life. If they are used to recognizing and communicating what is going on in their world, they may tell us, "I was mad and hit my friend at recess today," "I feel embarrassed that I'm not a good reader," or "I'm sad that my parents are getting a divorce." This is a good sign that they're developing an awareness of how they feel and confidence in expressing their feelings.

It is common or easy to stuff down our feelings, and this can create a sense of isolation. It takes time to practice these steps and may be easier for some than others. A great tool to help with this is to use an Emotions/Emoji Chart, like the one included in the appendix.

You may want to use the Emotions/Emoji Chart for yourself, sharing it with your spouse or a parenting partner, and also sharing it with a child or as a family.

Another tool that is helpful for sharing feelings, which is easy to remember, is IFAB: **I** - **F**eel (emotion) - **A**bout (situation) - **B**ecause (message).[81] For example, a child can say, "I feel sad about getting a bad grade on my test, because I worked really

---

[81] Riemersma, J. (2019). Pastoral Sex Addiction Professional (PSAP) Training. International Institute for Trauma & Addiction Professionals. February.

CHAPTER 4: FOSTER CONNECTION

hard on it, and I failed." Or, "I feel angry about my sister coming in my room, because she is not respecting my request. I feel disrespected." This tool can be used in so many ways. It is helpful to begin doing this yourself until it becomes a habit. When you are feeling an uncomfortable feeling, but you aren't quite sure why, it allows you to stop and think about what is really going on.

- "I feel overwhelmed about my finances because money problems remind me of mistakes I have made regarding money in the past."
- "I feel anxious and rejected about our sexual relationship, because I hear the message that I am a failure."

We can also use this tool with our children, so it becomes a more natural part of our language and communication.

There is a great animated movie called *Inside Out*.[82] It was a tear jerker for my wife and I, watching this with our son the day he moved away from home for the first time. Pixar did a great job bringing to life how emotions work in the brain. Sometimes feelings become the tail that wags the dog. Emotions can influence how we think and how we act. *Inside Out* is a great family movie to watch and discuss emotions. It's funny and endearing. It's a great portrayal of human emotions and the role they play in our lives: what's going on in our brain that explains what's happening in our behavior.

As parents, being willing to share our emotions, struggles, and mistakes builds trust with our children and models how they can share with us. This has been an amazing part of growth as

---

[82] Rivera, J. (Producer), & Docter, P. (Director). (2015). *Inside Out* [Motion Picture]. United States: Pixar Animation Studios.

parents for me and my wife—we now have regular conversations as a family about what we are thinking and feeling, insecurities and struggles we're having, as well as sharing the positive things going on in our world. Sometimes, as parents, it takes intentionally leading the way. This has been an ongoing process for us—it has opened up our family and our ability to share much deeper than we normally would have. This has created a great place of trust and safety. I wish my wife and I would have had the training to get to this sooner.

DISTRACTIONS

I'd like to say I always got this right, but distractions happen so often to parents and in so many ways. I didn't always fully understand the importance of being intentional about ongoing connection.

One of the true enemies of our parenting relationship is not being fully present with our kids because we are preoccupied with so many other things—worries, fears, schedules, appointments, finances, social media, obligations, and responsibilities—that we just miss being present.

Have you ever heard your kids say to you, "Dad. Dad. Dad,"(or mom) and it takes several times for them to get your attention? This happens to all of us.

I have admired my wife's natural ability to foster connection with our children. It seems to come easy for her. She's taught me so much about slowing down and learning to be present. I haven't always been able to figure out why being slowed down and present seems difficult for me. I have thought a lot about how I am wired, about having Attention Deficit Disorder, and about how I was raised. I've had to intentionally work hard at growing in this area.

CHAPTER 4: FOSTER CONNECTION

There were times when my kids were growing up that I missed opportunities to connect with them because I was so focused on my own issues, work, and interests, and wasn't always available to just be with them. Sometimes, as parents, we are still growing up ourselves and get caught up in our own fallout of trauma, relationships, and balancing the responsibilities of life.

For many parents, when we're busy building our careers or social lives, it can take our focus. Pursuing more "stuff" or financial security takes much of our energy and we have little left for our kids. Remember, we only have so many "energy units" to give and we choose daily where we will spend them.

I remember a season when I would come home from work after giving most of my energy at work and not saving much for when I came home. This was compounded by the fact that I'm an early riser and I'm generally winding down my day around 8:00 pm. I got in the habit of responding to my kids when they asked me to participate in something with the phrase, "I can't. I'm bushed."

I went on a family vacation once and my children were asking my wife and me about our dating years. My wife and I were sharing some stories and my wife said, "Your dad is a much better husband than he was a boyfriend because he is a lot more attentive to our relationship now." My youngest son Keaton, who was around five years old at the time, said, "He loved you, Mom. He was just bushed." My wife and I laughed when he said this, but it really impacted me. It woke me up to realize that I wasn't always doing a great job putting my energy toward connecting with my family. I didn't want my kids to remember, "My dad was a really hard worker, but he didn't have enough energy for us." Or, "My dad helped a lot of people, but he wasn't there for us." **BUILDING DEEP CONNECTION TAKES ENERGY AND INTENTIONALITY.**

These are a few mistakes I've made with raising my kids that I've had to process and grieve. In doing so, I have given myself permission and grace to grow and not be perfect. Admitting that I haven't been a perfect parent is scary, but in my experience, honesty and vulnerability, more often than not, lead to a deeper connection and greater intimacy in relationship.

QUALITY AND QUANTITY

Quality and quantity are both important. We can have a quality meal but not enough of it to sustain us. Quality time with our kids may not happen if we aren't available, especially as they move into their teenage years and become more interested in spending time with their peers than with their parents.

Look through your weekly schedule and ask yourself, "How much time have I prioritized spending time with my family and with my children?"

To change patterns and create more quality time with our kids may take intentional work over a period of time. We may have to retrain our brain in this area.

This is the benefit I have found in healthy support and group work—consistent change over time.

When our children are young they constantly want our attention and we can feel exhausted (I'm bushed). As they get older, they tend to get more independent, and as opportunities to connect become less, we have to be even more proactive.

I recently picked up chess with my sons again and when they were in the mood to play, I wanted to put aside whatever I was doing to stop and be present with them. I've also created a habit of sitting in the family room in the evening without the television on and letting conversation happen.

CHAPTER 4: FOSTER CONNECTION

It doesn't always come easily, but if we are aware, we can help cultivate many different opportunities for creating relationship with our kids.

TRADITIONS

Our traditions create a strong sense of family connection and endearment. They can happen on a daily or weekly basis, or they might be something that happens a few times a year, like a vacation or certain holidays. Growing up, one of my early connections with my family involved special times of meals around the table. A lot of good living happened around mealtime.

There is something about being part of something larger than ourselves that creates meaning in our lives. I am the youngest of five kids in the Wright family and we are up to 55 family members now, with grandkids and great grandkids. My niece made keychains for the family with our initial and the number of our birth order in the family. I am W-7: Wright family—member number seven. It is a powerful symbol of belonging. Growing up, my family made our annual family reunion a priority, which I never want to miss to this day. I grew up making great memories with extended family and my kids have grown up doing the same.

One of my favorite memories of connection with my son was at a family reunion when he was four years old. We were sitting out at a campground near a water spicket that had created a mud hole. Austin was playing and started to go near the mud. This made the older adults nervous and they started telling him, "Don't go near there, Austin. Go to your dad. You're going to get muddy." Since we were outside in our swimsuits anyway, I figured this was one of those times when the connection was more important than staying out of the mud. I took off my shirt and rolled around in the mud with him. The rest of the adults quickly went from concerned to laughing. I'm so glad I was mindful enough that day to choose the connection. The picture of us grinning and covered in mud hangs in my office to this day.

When we started raising a family, my wife and I talked about our personal observations of families who had created connectedness through traditions and shared experiences. For some families, this was through sporting events, yearly camping or backpacking trips, skiing on the weekends, birthday dinners, daily walks, and more. My wife and I have friends with five kids who created a tradition around ice cream sundaes on Sundays. These are different ways of building a strong connection to traditions. I have observed that children seem to connect to rituals, such as nightly bedtime stories, attending sporting events, or cherished holiday traditions. My wife's family has had many years of Thanks-ismas, where we celebrate most of the week of Thanksgiving and add in our Christmas traditions. Every year, we play all kinds of games, sing silly songs, and eat Aunt Shanny's scones for Christmas breakfast. Over the years, because of creating a sense of joy around this holiday, our children don't want to miss it. As adults, they will go to great lengths to not miss this week of family traditions.

AS OUR CHILDREN GROW OLDER, IT'S NORMAL FOR THEM TO PULL AWAY—OLD AND NEW RITUALS HELP KEEP THEM CONNECTED. Creating traditions doesn't have to be fancy or overwhelming, just something we do repetitively. For the last few years, I have made Saturday morning omelettes for my kids. This has been through a period of transition—from them living at home to moving out—and now they come over on Saturday mornings when they can.

CHAPTER 4: FOSTER CONNECTION

Sometimes these ideas and attempts to create tradition haven't gone so smoothly. We've had some huge camping trip fails with rain and mosquitoes. We didn't put our kids in every sport. We attempted a family devotion time for a season and during one such attempt people started getting frustrated with each other and stormed off to their different rooms. My wife and I were left sitting there saying, "Well, that went well." There was a season when our kids were teenagers where some of the family dynamics made it very difficult to do something all together as a family. My wife and I tried to do things one-on-one with them during this time—forgiving ourselves for not being able to live up to our own expectations and dreams of "family life." We constantly looked for what we called "wins" or some area where we could connect with each child at every stage of their growing up years, even the tough stages.

My wife and I recognized that many families grow up and become disconnected or have a lot of tension—we were trying to figure out how to create a dynamic that would draw our family together and cause our three kids and their future families to want to be with us. We began to sow some seeds and are still cultivating the right environment for this opportunity in their early adulthood.

Here are a few things we tried to do in our family:

- Create repetitive fun events, structured, minimizing the stress, and something our kids could count on.

- Have fun as a couple, model connection, and invite our kids to join us.

- Work on being other-centered, truly letting it go if they don't want to join us—not judging, guilting, or manipulating them to be a part.

- Model connection with our own parents and siblings, even when relationships are tough or we have differences.
- Be careful about not criticizing any family members to our kids.

My wife and I hope this will translate into healthy relationships with us, their siblings, and future family members as our family grows.

This isn't easy and, at times, takes humility and continued growth when we don't get it right. Sometimes, things happen that cause distance between us and our children.

If your children are older and there are some obstacles in your connection right now, begin to think of one thing that your children really enjoyed or that you have enjoyed together and make an effort to reestablish relationship. This might be an extra burden financially or relationally, but some amount of sacrifice is worth it. Painfully, it might also take backing off from the relationship, while letting your child know that the door is always open should they want to re-engage with you or the family. I believe in practicing the principle of "moving toward" when we can, sharing what we need, and setting appropriate boundaries.[83]

As parents, one of the things we need to remember is that no matter the age of our children or the missed opportunities when our children were young, we will always be their parent. Parenting continues throughout our children's lives. We cannot change the past, but we can start or continue today to foster connection by reaching out, writing a letter, or picking up the phone and expressing love and concern for them. It can take humility to be the first one to reach out, but we, as parents, should take the

---

[83] Riemersma, J. (2019). Pastoral Sex Addiction Professional (PSAP) Training. International Institute for Trauma & Addiction Professionals. February.

lead in this restorative process. **IN OUR FAMILIES AND OUR HOMES, WE SIMPLY HAVE TO BE AVAILABLE AND PRESENT FOR DAILY CONNECTION TO HAPPEN.**

TRIBAL ELDERS

My wife and I were talking about this chapter as we traveled to a week-long conference in Searcy, Arkansas, which was followed by a speaking engagement at a church in South Carolina. While there, we were impacted by a couple stories we heard from friends.

One of the conference speakers, Dr. Adrian Hickman, is the founder of Capstone Treatment Center for boys. He has decades of experience counseling and coaching others. My wife and I took a tour of the facility, where they have a 90-day program for young men ages 15-25. One part of their program is canine therapy. They've had great success with creating a bond and connection through the young men having their own puppy. The boys choose what color of puppy they would like and they take care of the puppy throughout their time in the program. They also take their puppy home with them.

Dr. Hickman shared that in their church community, when his boys were younger, the fathers would take turns teaching the kids, youth programs, and classes at church. This allowed the dads to connect with their sons and all the boys to learn from the different fathers.

A few days later, my wife and I were staying with some friends in South Carolina. They shared that when their boys were young, they would host a camp on their property, Camp Bohanon, every year. They set up obstacle courses and stations, such as hatchet throwing, archery, and a shooting range. They had a zipline through the woods, a fishing pond, and a variety of other outdoor events for boys to do with their fathers. They followed the day's activities with a big bonfire, a night of camping in sleeping bags, and then a pancake breakfast, making for a great experience. This was a great way for dads and sons to create connection and relationship.

These are two really valuable examples of how dads can stay involved in the lives of their kids. Finding ways to connect fathers with sons, especially during pre-adolescent years, is crucial to building relationship—boys learning from adult men what it means to grow into and become a healthy man.

Often in our culture and churches, our children spend most of the time with their peers. Even in our churches, we have young youth pastors and leaders who take on the responsibility of mentoring our kids.

I have developed some gray hair now, so I have been thinking a lot more about what it means to be a "tribal elder." I think it means passing on what we have learned and are learning to younger men and women. It means parents staying involved with their sons and daughters, not just socially, but emotionally. While it seems that women tend to come by relationships more naturally, there is a place for them to be vulnerable with their daughters and even their daughter's friends. For years, a friend of our family held a group in her home for her daughter and her daughter's friends from school. This mom took the time to teach all these young women life skills and values.[84]

These are several examples of individuals working hard to foster connection with the younger generation. I admire their work.

---

[84] Gilbert, K. (2015). Reclaiming Home: The Family's Guide for Life, Love and Legacy. New York, NY: Morgan James Publishing.

CHAPTER 4: FOSTER CONNECTION

Author Richard Rohr speaks about the need for tribal elders and the loss of initiation-type practices.[85]

> AT CERTAIN POINTS ALONG THE WAY, WE ARE PRONE TO GETTING STUCK UNLESS WE HAVE 1) SOME KIND OF INITIATORY EXPERIENCE, 2) SOME HEALING RITES OF PASSAGE, AND 3) ALMOST ALWAYS THE AID OF SOME GUIDES OR ELDERS.

For many of us, this is our opportunity, and even responsibility, to become these guides, challengers, and encouragers.

When we are challenged, it is hard to let go of what is comfortable or what we have held as "certain" in the past because the unknown and lack of control are scary to us. Western culture often encourages us to perform better or to do the "right" thing and pursue success.

Culture misses out on true elders who have done their own work and are present to lead us forward.

We have an opportunity. **WE CAN FIND WAYS TO HOLD ON TO AND CELEBRATE WHAT IS MEANINGFUL ABOUT MOVING FROM CHILDHOOD INTO ADULTHOOD.** We can create opportunities to connect with the younger generation and help them set a course. There is a confidence that comes from being surrounded by those who are older than us. Being surrounded by the women of our "village" and their influence isn't something that is completely lost.

---

[85] Rohr, R. (2015). *Native and Celtic Spirituality*. Retrieved from https://cac.org/initiation-2015-07-10/.

We can replicate this in our own ways:

- Including our children in activities we enjoy, are a part of, or are learning.
- Marking significant "rites of passage" around puberty or milestone birthdays can create some meaningful family traditions and deepen connection.
- Building traditions around specific interests in our child's life.
- As a parent, spending time with someone older than ourselves as a way of continued learning.

Think about the community you're in and how older men and women could be a bigger part of the training and mentoring of the youth. How can you celebrate with your daughters and sons as they move into adolescence? Are you a tribal elder now? If not, you will be. How can you influence the younger generation?

> YOU KNOW AFTER ANY TRULY INITIATING EXPERIENCE THAT YOU ARE PART OF A MUCH BIGGER WHOLE. LIFE IS NOT ABOUT YOU HENCEFORWARD, BUT YOU ARE ABOUT LIFE.[86]

---

[86] Rohr, R. (2004). *Adam's Return: The Five Promises of Male Initiation*. New York, NY: The Crossroad Publishing Company.

CHAPTER 4
TRY THIS!

THINK OF AN ACTIVITY YOUR CHILD HAS AN INTEREST IN AND SEE IF YOU COULD PARTICIPATE WITH THEM THIS WEEK.

OR

IN A CONVERSATION WITH YOUR FAMILY, ASK EACH PERSON TO SHARE THEIR FAVORITE FAMILY MEMORY THIS PAST YEAR.

QUESTIONS

1 | Think of a recent time where you were vulnerable. What did this feel like?

2 | Go to the Emotions/Emoji Chart in the appendix and choose three words that describe how you are feeling right now. Could you begin to use this worksheet with your spouse or children on a regular basis? When could you start?

3 | What is a significant experience in your family or your child's life this past year. What emotions did you feel regarding this experience (IFAB)?

4 | Do you have a ruptured relationship with a child or parent right now? What is something you could do to move toward reconciliation? (This could include appropriate boundaries expressed out of love).

CHAPTER 5

BE READY AT ANY TIME

It's not the "one talk" we have with our kids when they're a pre-teen, but rather the open and ongoing dialogue we provide whenever and wherever the opportunity arises. **Think about it this way: it's not about having the one 100-minute conversation; it's more about the 100 one-minute conversations.**[87] The previous chapters are so key: the intent is not to hurry the preparations for one conversation, but make sure we have done the work (at times, hard work) to connect with our kids. If we work through the previous chapters and lay the groundwork, then it becomes about practicing and being aware of opportunity. We can learn to cultivate daily practices, tools, and disciplines that contribute to how we communicate and help us to be more mindful—not only self-aware but aware of our interaction with others. This is about being proactive, not missing opportunities because we are looking for them. This is about living in the moment. Many times, what keeps us from living in the moment is worry and fear.

Mindfulness—awareness and being present—will help us be prepared ahead of time to **be ready at any time.**

---

[87] Roffman, D. (2001). *Sex and Sensibility: The Thinking Parent's Guide to Talking Sense About Sex.* Cambridge, MA: Perseus Publishing.

For me, sometimes mindfulness just means slowing down and being present in my life. This isn't something I necessarily grew up being aware of, but having daily practices has been a big part of my own personal health. There is an easy acrostic to remember about the **ART** of being present.[88]

- **Activities:** Bringing mindfulness into the everyday activities we are already doing.

- **Routines:** Building focused, slow routines into our day, which can be as easy as quiet time or exercise every morning.

- **Triggers:** When we are doing our own personal work, we become aware of things that set us off—creating anxiety, anger, fear—and we can use calming techniques, such as deep breathing and relaxation to bring our focus back to the present.

I used this last practice when my kids were young. On my way home from work, I would sometimes pull over the car and take some deep breaths, so I could be emotionally present, centering myself before I came in the door to the needs of my family. At the time, I didn't even really know this was mindfulness, but since then I have added several other tools that are especially helpful to me.

We want to build into our own lives and help our children build into their lives practices that support our deepest values such as family, community, relationship, service of others, care for ourselves, and love.

---

[88] Gimian, J. (2016). *How to Practice the Art of Being Present*. Retrieved from https://www.mindful.org/practice-art-being-present/.

CHAPTER 5: BE READY AT ANY TIME

JEWISH SHEMA

There is an ancient text in the Hebrew Scriptures that speaks about this concept first hand.

> ⁴THE LORD OUR GOD, THE LORD IS ONE. ⁵LOVE THE LORD YOUR GOD WITH ALL YOUR HEART AND WITH ALL YOUR SOUL, AND WITH ALL YOUR STRENGTH. ⁶THESE COMMANDMENTS THAT I GIVE YOU TODAY ARE TO BE ON YOUR HEARTS. ⁷IMPRESS THEM ON YOUR CHILDREN. TALK ABOUT THEM WHEN YOU SIT AT HOME AND WHEN YOU WALK ALONG THE ROAD, WHEN YOU LIE DOWN AND WHEN YOU GET UP. ⁸TIE THEM AS SYMBOLS ON YOUR HANDS AND BIND THEM ON YOUR FOREHEADS. ⁹WRITE THEM ON THE DOORFRAMES OF YOUR HOUSES AND ON YOUR GATES.[89]

Some people may take this passage of Scripture more literally and will have practices such as family devotions, prayer, Scripture memory and other disciplines. These are all really valuable and the different ways of walking this out will be effective for different families.

The big picture: we are using all different situations in our day-to-day living to impart our values to our children and help them mature. The concept here is about seizing the opportunity to talk to our kids at different points along their journey. This speaks to being equipped ourselves in order to help our kids learn. **Personal health, educating ourselves, fostering connection, and practicing our communication**—before we get there—will make these opportunities more natural and relational.

---

[89] Deuteronomy 6:4-9

You may be reading this book today not because of a question your child has already asked, but in preparation for when the time comes that requires a response.

Being equipped is the best way to be ready. I have always been appreciative of those who are first responders in our country, such as firefighters, medical personnel, or law enforcement. They regularly train, practice, and prepare by simulating responses to potential situations, so at any time, day or night, when there is a call for help, they are ready to respond. This is a type of mental rehearsal.

Roleplaying and mental rehearsal are effective ways to make ourselves more comfortable with the language and topics around sexuality that aren't often discussed but are very important. This is why we need to practice ongoing dialog with someone else, out loud, before the time comes to share with our kids.

Sometimes we push aside the importance because of the discomfort. The more we practice, the more we normalize the topics and conversations, the less uncomfortable it is. Even when the time comes to talk about it, it will be most awkward early on, and it will get easier, even if it remains an uncomfortable area of life to talk about. It's okay to lean into this discomfort.

Being ready is about being mentally and emotionally ready, as well as physically present and available. Having a mental focus and understanding of what we want to teach our children requires some learning. **BEING EMOTIONALLY HEALTHY OURSELVES REQUIRES PERSONAL WORK AND SELF-CARE.** Being physically present and available requires choice and evaluating our priorities and the values we are actually living out, so we can keep embracing them or so we can make changes. All of this requires living intentionally.

To many adults, in a wide range of settings, from couples counseling to parent trainings, I have asked the question, "How

CHAPTER 5: BE READY AT ANY TIME

many of you had open conversations with your parents about sexuality?" The majority had little to no conversation. It wasn't so much that there was a lack of opportunity, but more that the occasion was missed. The moment came, but the parents weren't ready to seize it.

As I reflect on this, it reminds me that if we wait until our children are older to start the conversation, it may never happen.

You have the choice right now to start the conversation wherever you're at—regardless of your children's age. The opportunity is still there for initiating conversation.

AVAILABILITY

Think of it like this: when we merge onto a freeway, we get ready. We look, and we keep looking, and then take the opportunity when the time comes. In training our children, this is about putting ourselves in the place of just being there. It's hard to have teachable moments if we aren't present and available. This can look like working on a science project even when we aren't good at putting things together, being a counselor at a kids camp, or the every day simple things like just being in the same room with our teenagers until they are ready to talk. Often, all of these times of just being available, when no conversation happens, prepares us for the occasional "big" moments when our child opens up.

Sometimes we don't realize how a small thing to us could be a big thing to our child. I have worked on this and continue to work on being present, just sitting in the same room as my kids until the conversation happens—being aware of moments when they are ready to talk.

This isn't easy for me, but I have come to think of it as a skill we can learn. I am, by nature, independent, an extrovert, and I have Attention Deficit Disorder. I am distracted a lot and most of all by interacting with, talking to, and meeting the needs of people. I enjoy conversation and building relationship with a whole bunch of people, where my wife is more naturally "deep with a few." This has worked well for us sometimes and has been a struggle at other times.

I'm also not very confident in putting things together or doing "projects." Sometimes my mechanical inabilities kept me from engaging in more projects with my sons. I wish I was more this way, but I'm not. It's easy for me to say "no" to things I don't feel I'm good at or things that take a lot of focus.

A few years ago, when my son was 19 years old, he wanted to move to the Seattle area. He had done an internship there, and, in true millennial style, decided to sell all of his earthly possessions for a more minimalist lifestyle. He bought an SUV that he could put a mattress in and decided to move into a car community at a large church. He detailed his car and organized it. My wife called him the cleanest homeless person she has ever met. One snowy Saturday, before he left, he came in and asked, "Dad, I got cardboard to cut out around my windows, so that it stays warm at night. Would you come outside and help me cut them out?" The answer to whether I "wanted to" was no. I really didn't want to go outside in the cold, but I could tell he wanted me to be with him, so I did. Three hours later, after cutting cardboard in the garage to fit every window, we were finished. I left doing what I "felt" like doing, watching a football game in a warm house, and ended up with the opportunity to be available for connection and accomplishing something with my son. A few weeks later, I got this random text from my son, now in Seattle: "I'm thankful for a dad who cuts out cardboard with his son in the cold."

CHAPTER 5: BE READY AT ANY TIME

TEACHABLE MOMENTS

Not every moment is a teachable moment, and not every teachable moment has to be spontaneous. Sometimes, teachable moments can be planned and anticipated. Every child will not automatically be open about their questions and concerns. Preparing for when we are going to share about puberty or the act of sex might be needed.

Throughout this book, I recommend resources which are age-appropriate, that parents can read or view with their kids and discuss together. Many of these resources start at the early ages of understanding and continue into adulthood. These resources can help cultivate a planned conversation.

Sometimes teachable moments happen because we create the environment to make them more comfortable. For example, taking one of our kids for a one-on-one weekend away and getting out of our routine and environment, with the intention of bringing up conversation around sexuality.

I shared about doing this with my sons when they were in middle school. Leaving town and spending a couple of travel days together in the car, provided uninterrupted time with them, intentional time to focus on talking about their growth in adolescence, and unstructured time to value the relationship.

We know that preadolescents and teenagers are not always ready for a conversation of any kind.[90] This is why fostering a connection and creating opportunities for conversation in small pieces is so important. If we sit down at a table across from our child and try to have a serious conversation, it will probably be much less received than having the conversation while riding in the car

---

[90] Culture Reframed (2019). *Parents of Tweens.* Culture Reframed Parents Program. Retrieved from https://parents.culturereframed.org/course/parents-of-tweens/.

for a period of time, taking a walk or hiking, baking something or making a snack in the kitchen together. There are many small ways to position ourselves and be ready for conversation where the focus isn't directly on the conversation. Even while we are watching television, be ready for the opportunities (and there are many) to explain or ask our child what they think about situations that are portrayed in television shows, movies, and ads.

Teachable moments can come out of witnessing or observing right or wrong actions, whether these are our own actions, our child's, or the actions of others. We could be watching the news and new allegations of sexual misconduct come up. We can observe with our child someone being disrespectful to others. Our child may tell us they saw pornography at a friend's house and handled it well or didn't. These are all potential teachable moments.

A teachable moment that I remember clearly happened to me in the eighth grade at my junior high school in Modesto, California. It was a small private school. I was with my teacher and class when we were passing through the hall right outside of Mr. Clark's office, the principal. Someone was giving us instructions and the group was having a difficult time listening or following the instructions. The teacher was trying to get our attention and just when she began to get us to focus, I shouted out a smart remark, making everyone laugh. Little did I know, the principal had just walked up behind me and heard the comment I made. Seizing the moment, he tapped on my shoulder and said, "Would you please come with me?" He opened the door to his office and asked me to be seated. I can still see the look on my friend's faces as I walked away. You're busted!

Mr. Clark began to speak in a very calm voice and said something to me that I've never forgotten to this day: "Rodney, in life you don't always have to be funny and you don't always need to have the last word. I hope you remember this conversation and take to heart what I am telling you, not just for today, but for the rest of your life." I was about 13 years old at the time and, at times, I still can hear him saying those words.

Correction that is a teaching moment and not a shaming moment impacts us in a powerful way. We often teach our kids through correction and instruction. **SOMETIMES, THE BEST TEACHABLE MOMENTS COME FROM CATCHING OUR KIDS DOING SOMETHING RIGHT AND AFFIRMING THEM.**

Over the years, my wife and I have made a practice of affirming our children in front of other parents, family members, and teachers. We also affirm other children and young adults to their parent or a teacher, in front of them.

Positive reinforcement sticks with all of us in a powerful way.

DISCERNMENT

In recognizing the importance of training our children, we can try so hard that we damage or lose some of the relationship in the process. Knowing when emotions are too high, and when we may want to choose another setting or time to make our point, takes wisdom and discernment. Our child may not be ready for the conversation. Every child is different in how they respond to what we are trying to say.

SOMETIMES IN OUR NEED TO GET IT RIGHT, WE MISS THE HEART OF OUR CHILD. Our intention is good, but we can end up polarizing or creating walls. Be aware of overkill.

Discernment is key. The teachable moment isn't just when we dispense information, but when our child hears it, understands it, and receives it. It may actually sink in later. Many conversations will be short. Small amounts of information on more frequent occasions is very beneficial. These moments are around us all the time, if we are aware. They can take the shape of a long dialogue between us and our child, or can simply be a short statement, with eye contact, where we know the message was received.

FAMILY DISCLOSURE

Sometimes significant things happen in a family that, at some point, we may want to share with our children. Timing is important when we are sharing potentially sensitive information. There is value in having them hear it from us rather than someone else or accidentally discovering information, such as an affair or a parent being in a previous marriage. There is also value in our children knowing we made mistakes along the way in our journey and corrected them or have learned from them. While we are raising kids, we are often still learning from these mistakes and growing in our own understanding and maturity. It's amazing how we, and even our kids, can think that we are "the adult," so we should have it all figured out.

At times, parents worry about sharing their history with their kids, because they are afraid of either the shame or of it somehow giving the child "permission" to make the same or similar mistakes. In my experience, the opposite is most often true. **WHEN WE CREATE A PLACE OF VULNERABILITY, WE ARE SAFE PEOPLE TO CONFIDE IN WHEN OUR CHILDREN ARE STRUGGLING.** We actually have the opportunity to explain the reason behind our values and actions.

My wife and I had conversations about how we would share my story of sexual addiction and our journey of healing with our kids. We chose to share it with them later in their teenage years. In hindsight, we think it would have been better to share

CHAPTER 5: BE READY AT ANY TIME

it even earlier, so that conversation would have been opened all the more about their own sexuality and questions. Our concern was based on the timing and ages of all our children, as well as personal things they were going through. Sometimes when a child is dysregulated in their own life or dealing with trauma, it can take discernment to know the timing to share with them. Our heart wasn't to lay a heavy burden on our children. We were sensitive to when they were walking through their own emotional situations navigating the younger teenage years, but also wanted to let them know we have struggled. We wanted to be an anchor for them to grab onto. There isn't one right way of doing this, but our vulnerability earlier could have fostered more conversation and helped them to see that there aren't "taboo" subjects in our home. Another reason to have open conversations about sexuality and pornography throughout their growing up years is so that when we share something from our own story, our child already has plenty of narrative surrounding the subject of sexuality.

A note about disclosure: disclosure is an important part of the process but is something that should be handled with wisdom. Seeking counsel from a spouse, friends, or trained experts is helpful in determining the right timing and approach in sharing with your family, depending on what you are disclosing. This would be especially true if your child has experienced significant trauma in their life. It's important that parents discuss this with each other and find the right time and way to disclose to their kids.

Disclosure can be scary, and it can produce emotional reactions in those we share with, but it is often the healthy thing to do. When it comes to disclosure, "It sometimes gets worse before it gets better." The right thing to do is often the hard thing to do.[91] Everyone has a different way of handling things emotionally. Kids can be affected in different ways and have different reactions. They may become shut down or have a lot of questions. They may be angry or seem indifferent. We want to be ready for however they respond, without over or underreacting to them. Validate that they may need time to process, but that, "Your mom and I are open to having more conversation."

You might say, "I can see this has really impacted you. Your mom and I have emotions around it as well." Give your child time to process and let them know that they can come back with questions. If they don't come back to you, bring it up again within a few days and create an opportunity for more conversation.

BEING SHOCKPROOF

Sometimes our children's behavior or words can come across as shocking to us. In many instances our children may use words, expressions, or actions that take us by surprise. If we are prepared and ready for these situations, we can address them without being shocked and our child feeling "shamed." **There may be times when our child wants to open up about very private or sensitive thoughts or experiences and they want to see if we are an emotionally safe person to share this with.** Our reaction to them is often bigger than we even realize. The biggest key is having an appropriate response to what they say or do that establishes trust and safety.

My friend told me a story about when he was an adolescent. He was riding in the back of the car with his father, sitting in the backseat with his parents up front. He said to his dad, "I've been

---

[91] Dye, M. (2012). *The Genesis Process: For Change Groups, Book 1 and 2, Individual Workbook* (4th ed.). Auburn, CA: Michael Dye.

CHAPTER 5: BE READY AT ANY TIME

having a lot of wet dreams lately. Did you have a lot of those when you were my age?" He said he caught his dad's eye in the rearview mirror, and his dad looked shocked and embarrassed and quickly said, "No, no I didn't." A silent awkwardness fell across the car. From his perspective, this wasn't a safe topic to continue.

At times, we make a mistake or respond in a way we wish we hadn't. If we don't like the way we have responded to something, we can go back and talk about it and even apologize for our response, if appropriate. This gives our child a new experience with us and the situation. New opposite experiences are a powerful part of how we change as human beings.[92] **IF WE HAVE THE OPPORTUNITY TO CHANGE, THEN WE HAVE THE OPPORTUNITY TO RECONNECT.**

The organization, Culture Reframed, has a great website full of resources for parents. They have a section to prepare parents to be shockproof for when their children look at porn called COMPOSE Yourself—we have included the link to this in our resource list in the appendix. It is completely normal to have a range of emotions when our child views porn or participates in something porn-related. One of the great points Culture Reframed makes is that if our first response is anger, it should be directed at the porn industry, not at our child.[93] Pornography companies are strategically marketing to our kids at younger and younger ages. There are so many types of situations that can come up and we want to be ready to hear anything from our child and know generally how we are going to choose to respond to it. Our natural reactions often come from the emotional part

---

[92] Ibid.

[93] Dines, G. (2019). COMPOSE Yourself! Retrieved from https://www.culturereframed.org/compose-yourself/.

of our brain (limbic) that overrides the logical, thinking part of our brain.[94] The emotional and logical parts of our brain can work together to respond more closely to the way we would like. It's always better to respond than react.

One evening, my youngest son and I were watching a football game and talking, and he used the word "bitch." I paused the television and asked him if he knew what that word meant? He said, "No." He had just heard it at school. I took the opportunity to let him know that it comes from the word for a female dog, but unfortunately, it's used in a degrading way toward women at times, and that it would never be kind to refer to anyone in that way.

At times, I've been known to use shock value as a teaching tool. I started telling him all of the cuss words I could think of and how they are used and misused, as degrading comments toward others. I wanted this to be a teaching tool, to make him aware that language matters and, in my opinion, profanity is the lowest form of communication. Words are just words and aren't bad in themselves—what makes them bad is the way in which we use them. We spent the next several minutes talking about a number of cuss words that we don't regularly use and how they could be seen as degrading to others. I recognized that as he grew into an adult, he would be making the decisions as to what language he would choose to use. I wouldn't be controlling this, but I could influence him.

I wanted my son to understand that the heart and intention behind the words we use really matters. Our conversation was not about being shocked with his behavior, but about informing him.

Many times, my wife and I used being shockproof when the kids would ask about tattoos or tongue-piercing and conversations

---

[94] Therapists Aid LLC (2015). The Wise Mind. TherapistAid.com. Retrieved from https://www.therapistaid.com/worksheets/wise-mind.pdf.

about boyfriends or girlfriends. We tried not to automatically give our kids direct answers for things we wanted them to think about and talk about the decision together. My wife made an effort at being shockproof when Walmart called and our youngest son had decided to shoplift something with a friend. She arrived at Walmart to hear from the manager that it "looks like your son doesn't do this often, because he's not very good at it," but they did require him to pay a fine that came out of his own pocket. This gave him a natural consequence for the choice. Lesson learned. My wife used a quiet approach that day—picking him up and just letting him know that this made her sad. She didn't really know what to say. Our son already knew the choice was wrong and what we would think about it. This was a time where her approach allowed her to be a part of future confidences and conversations with our son.

Our other son wanted to know if he could have a girlfriend when he was in the sixth grade. Instead of giving him a yes-or-no answer, my wife explored with him what it meant to have a girlfriend at his stage of life. They came to an understanding on the subject and she let him make the decision. It didn't really last long. It seemed a little more effort than he wanted to make, but the ability to not overreact and to let it be a shared decision was appropriate and helpful in this situation. **MANY SITUATIONS WILL DIFFUSE THEMSELVES IF WE ENGAGE OUR KIDS IN CONVERSATION AND DON'T OVERREACT.**

MISSED OPPORTUNITIES

It is always nice when we are mentally or emotionally ready for a situation or a question to arise, although this hasn't always been the case for me.

I remember a time of camping with my two sons when they were young. We went up to Farragut State Park in North Idaho and set up our tent at the south end of Pend Oreille Lake. We collected some firewood for the evening and we were cooking chili for dinner (aka, opening a can and warming it on the burner). The setting was right. Father and his boys unplugging from television and technology, being outside in nature, learning to build a campfire—just being together. Over dinner we were having great campfire conversation, when the conversation turned toward sex and a question was asked about pornography. One of my sons said, "Dad, have you ever looked at porn?" What a great question for a son to ask his father. It was a perfect time to have an honest conversation.

Unfortunately, I was still living with the shame from my sexual addiction. Although I had established long-term sobriety, I didn't have emotional healing from the shame. My wife and I had not yet disclosed to our family. I wasn't ready because I hadn't fully worked through my own mistakes and the shame surrounding it. When my son asked this question, here is what I started to feel: fear, anxiety, uncertainty, shame, and an overwhelming thought of wanting to be somewhere else other than here with my boys (isolation). So, do you know what I said? I turned to my boys and said, "Who wants more chili?" I immediately changed the subject and went on to something else. The whole exchange lasted maybe 30 seconds, but to me, it seemed like an eternity.

Talk about a missed opportunity. What I wish I would have said is, "Yes, I have struggled with pornography in the past, and it has brought a lot of pain and hurt in my life and others, including your mother, and here is why pornography isn't the better way…"

CHAPTER 5: BE READY AT ANY TIME

I share this with you for two reasons:
1. We have to get healing from our shame.
2. We won't always get it right.

I don't have time to make all the mistakes, and neither do you—so we have to learn from others. Please let my missed opportunity be your opportunity to be ready when your "Who wants more chili" question comes.

When I have talked to my boys about this story, now that they're adults, they remember camping but not this part of the conversation. But guess who does remember it? ME! I will never forget it because of the way it was attached to my shame. I had a great opportunity to answer their question directly and create a road to further questions from them in this area.

I thank God that parenting isn't a one-time shot at getting it right or wrong, but an ongoing opportunity for learning. Had I worked through my own healing process sooner, I would have been ready for their question. This would have been a great opportunity.

The truth is, there are many opportunities that my wife and I missed. My wife has also gone back to our daughter to apologize and say, "I'm sorry that I missed some opportunities to initiate conversation with you in certain areas around sexuality. I see now that I probably wasn't ready for some of the questions that may have come up. Because you were making good decisions, I sometimes overlooked this area of parenting you. I believe that more conversation around what questions you might have had was a missed opportunity of connection for both of us."

Missed opportunities are a part of being human and being parents. But there will always be future opportunities to pick up from right where we're at, learn, and apply truth in new ways.

CHAPTER 5
TRY THIS!

REVIEW THE FIRST FOUR CHAPTERS TO SEE HOW MUCH YOU HAVE PREPARED YOURSELF TO BE READY AT ANY TIME.

AND

CHOOSE A TIME AND PLACE TO JUST BE AVAILABLE WITH YOUR KIDS, WHETHER CONVERSATION HAPPENS OR NOT.

QUESTIONS

1 | When you look at your parenting, how easily does "being ready at any time" work for you?

2 | What experiences come to mind where you were either prepared or not for a teachable moment?

3 | What do you think about being shockproof? What does "being shockproof" mean to you?

4 | Reread the ART of being present on page 100. How do your activities, routines, and triggers support your ability to be present?

CHAPTER 6

WELCOME QUESTIONS

"Dad, is it true that babies come out of mom's vagina?" I'll never forget this question that came from the mouth of my five-year-old son, sitting in the back seat of our red Dodge minivan as we were driving back from the Oregon coast. My wife had fallen asleep next to me, but she was awake now. The word vagina had just come flying through the van. Looking in the rearview mirror, I responded with, "Yep, that's how God made it. Babies come out of what's called the birth canal, and they come right out of the mom's vagina." I heard his sister hit him in the arm gently and say, "See, I told you, Austin!" Whitney, his older and wiser by a year sister, had previously had the conversation with Mom about where babies come from. As I continued the conversation with Austin, I looked at him and said, "When moms have babies it really, really hurts, and even though there's a lot of joy, it's very painful. I'm sure glad God made me a boy." His eyes got as big as saucers, and then he looked at his sister and said, "Me too, Dad, 'Sorry about that, Whitney!'" His response was as if to say, "Someday you're going to have all this pain sister. Dad just said." It was such an endearing conversation.

Isn't it cool when the family of origin becomes a place where it's okay to ask questions?

This may be one of our biggest fears as parents: "What if my child asks a question and I don't know the answer?" None of us know the answers to every question and giving the perfect answer every time isn't the goal. We aren't born with the wisdom and understanding of how things work. It's a gradual process of learning. **CREATING A CONNECTION WHERE OUR KIDS KNOW THAT THEY CAN ASK MOM AND DAD QUESTIONS, AND THE QUESTIONS WILL BE WELCOMED, IS ONE OF THE BEST WAYS TO STAY CONNECTED AND EDUCATE.**

Kids seem to ask the most interesting questions, but in reality this is how we all learn. Most young children will ask questions like:

- How are babies made?
- How does a baby get in a mommy's tummy?
- Why does my penis get hard?
- Why do girls have different parts than boys?

Younger kids don't know not to ask questions. They may ask you all kinds of things. "How does this work? Why this and why that?" Young kids are very curious. Every child has a different personality and some children seem more curious than others.

My wife and I have one son who wanted to know everything and would process with us. Another one of our sons is a deep contemplator. He doesn't always express what he is thinking about, but he thinks deeply. Our daughter takes life as it comes and is pretty even keel most of the time. When she was young, she always wanted to know what was coming and the structure of the day, so she would ask a hundred questions about what we were doing tomorrow and then let everyone know: "We are going to the grocery store and then to see grandma, and then we might play a game…!"

CHAPTER 6: WELCOME QUESTIONS

Curiosity generally grows from a safe and familiar environment.[95] When the setting feels safe and familiar, we seek new experiences. When we feel overwhelmed, we seek familiarity. Kids learn best when they're trying to get the answers to their own question. They gain more information, learn it better, and retain it longer. They gain a deeper understanding. Author Susan Engel states, "Curiosity is the engine that fuels learning."[96] She says that when our kids are interested they learn better, for longer, learn more, and gain a deeper understanding from it.

Studies have shown that most young children ask between 25 and 50 questions an hour.[97] As parents, many of us have experienced this. We get used to hearing all the questions and sometimes, after the fiftieth question in an hour, we think, *Is this kid ever going to stop?* If we are distracted and not used to being mindful and paying attention, we hope to answer quickly. If we have a number of jobs, tasks to do, and/or multiple other children, it can feel pretty time-consuming to be present with our curious child day after day.[98]

We may notice how children's curiosity lessens as they get older. The continuation of curiosity comes in part from the responses they receive from those around them and even seeing adults ask questions.[99]

---

[95] Perry, B. (2019). *Why Young Children Are Curious.* Scholastic. Retrieved from https://www.scholastic.com/teachers/articles/teaching-content/why-young-children-are-curious/.

[96] Engel, S. (2015). *The Hungry Mind: The Origins of Curiosity in Childhood.* Cambridge, MA: Harvard College.

[97] Ibid.

[98] Altschuler, G. (2015). *Are Kids Curious?* Psychology Today. Retrieved from https://www.psychologytoday.com/us/blog/is-america/201502/are-kids-curious.

[99] Engle, S. (2011). *The Hungry Mind: The Origins of Curiosity.* WilliamsCollege. Retrieved from https://www.youtube.com/watch?v=Wh4WAdw-oq8.

I chose to raise my children not just handing out what I thought the "right" or moral answer was to every question but asking the questions along with them. This is good because it let them know I don't have all of the answers figured out. I'm still curious and asking questions to this day. Kids need plenty of time to explore problems and ask any question that might come to them. As parents, this is our opportunity to make it clear that "having the right answer is not the most important goal."[100]

Kids are very perceptive to the reactions they receive. If a parent is open and comfortable, kids will be also and, chances are, they will continue to ask questions. If kids perceive their parents' or another adult's discomfort—the emotional response or reaction they get from an adult—this will naturally affect how open they are in the future, especially if they perceive the questions or behaviors to be shameful or embarrassing. If the latter is the case, as they get older, they will ask less and less questions or just stop asking altogether.

This is why starting the conversation when our kids are younger is so important. As middle schoolers our kids are more apt to look to their peers when they have questions or to Google it. If they don't talk with us about it, they will find the answers somewhere else: from a friend, movies, or culture. This means they will often get a lot of wrong information.

I've observed among parents who start with comfortable conversations with their children at a young age, it gives them an easier platform, or base, to work from.

If you are starting this process with your kids late in the game, or you have a more quiet or introverted child, you may actually

---

[100] Altschuler, G. (2015). *Are Kids Curious?* Psychology Today. Retrieved from https://www.psychologytoday.com/us/blog/is-america/201502/are-kids-curious.

CHAPTER 6: WELCOME QUESTIONS

need to be the one who starts asking the questions. You can't assume that because they aren't asking a question, they don't have one. Whether early or late, it could be that you and your child are starting a process of learning these things together.

Ask, "Do you have any questions?" isn't usually the most effective way to start the conversation. Most likely they will say No. This was the primary "old school" way of navigating this and it didn't work very well. Parents would often hand their child a book (if even that) or try to have one awkward "birds and bees" talk, and then say, "Let me know if you have any questions." The parent was pretty much hoping, as much as the child was, that this was their last conversation about it.

Our culture is much more sexualized and open now, so our children are not going to get around the subject. They want someone to help with the constant messages that are coming at them, even if they can't articulate it.

Approaching your child creates opportunities for the questions to come up or for you to begin opening up. One of the best ways, if you haven't already cultivated this openness, is to start by sharing some vulnerable pieces of your own history—something you struggled with or a question you had, which is age-appropriate. Leading with our own story or questions you had growing up helps cultivate the conversation. Here is how this could happen: recall the question you had growing up, that maybe you did or didn't ask. Such as, "When I was a kid I always wondered if..." or "I asked my mom about _____, and she got embarrassed."

This place of vulnerability doesn't have to be about sexuality. You are just establishing a connection and creating openness. You are also building a foundation for questions, building up to the more mature questions as your children get older. You can cultivate questions using everyday situations, the teachable moments.

I have shared about reading with your children. This is one of the easiest ways to open up questions with younger children. From the very first time you start reading books with your kids, let one of the books be about anatomy. Build on this by discussing TV, movies, conversations you've overheard, or things going on at school.

COMMUNICATION

When it comes to communication, one parent may be more open conversationally, more equipped, or in a more healthy place to respond to their child's questions. Parents who are separated will need to have a plan around this, whether they communicate well with the co-parent or not. Also, communication doesn't need to include both parents. We can have the conversation individually. Whether we are single, separated, or married parents, we all need each other.

WE ARE BETTER TOGETHER! PEOPLE WHO PARENT, LEAD, SUCCEED, OR FAIL DIFFERENTLY THAN US ARE VALUABLE FOR OUR LIVES AND THE LIVES OF OUR CHILDREN.

Lean on others who you choose as parenting partners with you: family members, church leaders, or your small group. Invite trusted people in your world to support you in these conversations. Encourage your children to talk to and ask questions of other people in their lives. This is a great conversation to have with your children, to establish which relationships would be best and the parameters around confidentiality. Whether it's an aunt, youth leader, or family friend, allow your children space to keep safe confidences with other trusted adults.

One of my children confided in their aunt and said, "Thanks. I feel safe with you because you remind me of my mom in many ways." What a compliment to both their aunt and my wife.

CHAPTER 6: WELCOME QUESTIONS

Through the years, I've had many parents come to me and say, "Rodney, I need help with..." Sometimes, parents need a third party or even need help communicating their thoughts and feelings, depending on where they are at in their own lives.

It's important to be equipped to talk with your children, but don't think you have to be the "Superhero." You may be able to bring in a family member, friend, or counselor to help with difficult conversations and bring an outside objective voice.

CREATING SAFETY AND TRUST

As a parent, the foundation of our relationship with our child is always from a place of trust, which creates safety. **ONE OF THE BEST WAYS TO CREATE SAFETY AND TRUST IS TO TRULY CARE ABOUT WHAT OUR CHILD THINKS AND HOW THEY FEEL.** Beyond listening and speaking to them, also consider the environment where we are participating in something together. We need to create environments that produce safety and comfort for our children.

On a weekly basis, I used to take my son out to McDonald's to work on his spelling words. For those of you who know me personally, you might guess that we were both learning to improve our spelling at the same time. This time with my son was comfortable, repetitive, and in a nonthreatening environment.

We talked earlier about being ready for opportunities, but questions come up in these settings. Whether it's at the dinner table, throwing a football back and forth, walking the dog, or shopping together. These are all environments that could create a comfortable experience and open up questions.

Here are a few things that help create safety and trust:

LISTEN MORE THAN YOU TALK

Being a good listener is a skill I've had to learn and develop. One of the tools that helped me become a better listener is called active listening.[101] It simply means listening and then restating to the individual what you heard. For example, if your child asks you about some friends at school that they're having a difficult time with, you could respond, "So, it sounds like you are concerned about some things your friends at school are doing?" Or, "So there are kids at your school whose actions are causing a struggle for you?"

Sometimes, because of our own discomfort, we don't allow room for silence.

Some personalities will naturally overtalk or jump in with their own thoughts. I'll have to be honest, I've been guilty of overtalking from time to time.

Learn the skill of listening. Less is more.

NONVERBALS

When it comes to our nonverbal communication, watch your facial expressions and body language. This is why I recommend having the conversations with your spouse, friend, or small group before you attempt to address these topics and questions with your child.

Some things our kids come up with are a little shocking, even when we're the adult. Our face and body language will show how comfortable we are with the questions. This is where becoming a bit shockproof comes in handy. Our kids will pick up on our frozen stare, big eyes, embarrassed facial expression, or the steam coming out of our ears.

If you overreact, don't worry, it probably won't be the last time, and it's great to just address it. "Wow, your question really

---

[101] Prepare Enrich Training.

took me by surprise!" "Hmm, let me think about that for a minute." Or, after picking yourself up off the floor, "Could you repeat the question?" With some really open kids, you want to make sure you heard them right!

NOT HAVING ALL THE ANSWERS

If the parent is okay with not knowing the answer, the child learns that it's okay for them not to know the answer as well. A parent who has high expectations either has to keep up appearances for themselves (perfectionistic) or the child will see them as incompetent. Children see through facades. It's better to be honest and authentic.

We don't need to have all the right answers and never be wrong. Again, then we get the opportunity to grow along with our kids and their trust in us is built because they see our authenticity. Our authenticity matters to our kids. They are looking for what's real and tend to see through charades.

Parents, embrace humility! "Fake it 'til you make it" is not a good principle here. **No parent has all the right answers all the time!**

It's okay to say, "That's a great question. What do you think the answer to that question is?" At least, while they're answering, it gives you a few more seconds to think about how you want to respond to your child in the moment.

If you don't have a good answer, let your child know, "I'll have to think about it" and that you will come back to the question. If you answer something wrong or don't like the answer you gave, come back and address it. For example, "I was thinking about our conversation the other day and I misspoke."

Some questions we don't really ever have the answer to and this is okay. It's not always simple. There are confusing situations and experiences that are hard to completely understand. It's okay to learn that we don't need to have it all figured out and we can still trust.

The truth is, parents are going to have their own abundance of questions. This is where educating ourselves comes into play. Welcoming questions is a two-way street. If we welcome a question first, our kids will be more open to questions.

Here's a regret I had to correct with my boys that I shared in the last chapter: when we were camping and they first asked, "Dad have you ever looked at porn?" and I answered, "Who wants more chili?" It took me years to go back and correct this conversation with them. I reminded them of the story and apologized for avoiding the question because of my shame.

Sometimes you'll answer the question and feel like you nailed it, and sometimes you'll say, "Oh boy, I completely missed it on that one."

OPEN-ENDED QUESTIONS

What does it mean to ask an open-ended question?[102] It's a coaching type of question. It's about discovery. You've invited your child to share what they think or what they are learning. It helps them open up and process through conversation to say: "Here was my experience and this is how it affected me." It is like having a debrief with your child.

We are more apt to adopt something as our own if we self-discover it. There is nothing wrong with Yes or No questions, but they don't generally lead us to opening up more. Open-ended questions generally start with "How...?" "What...?" and sometimes "Why...?" "Why" questions can be open-ended,

---

[102] Grace Network International Training (2014). Creating Environments of Grace.

CHAPTER 6: WELCOME QUESTIONS

but can more easily put someone on the defensive. "How" or "What" questions are more disarming.

Here are several examples of how to engage your child with open-ended questions:

"Did you look at that image on the screen?" This is a Yes or No question.

"Why did you look at that image on the screen?" This might make them defensive and it can be hard for us to determine why we did something when it involves a mistake.

- What did you see on your screen?
- How did it make you feel when you saw that image on the screen?
- What did you think about what you saw...?
- How did you respond after you saw the image on the screen?
- What would you think if that was a picture of your mom, sister, or daughter?
- What message do you think that was sending?
- How do you think porn could be harmful for you?

This may be one way to help them open up and share.

Here's how a conversation might sound: Did you hit your brother? (yes or no.) Why did you hit your brother. ("Why" question.) What are you feeling right now? What made you angry at your brother? How do you feel about the way you responded? (Open-ended.)

You can see the difference between these questions. Open-ended questions invite more conversation and invite the person to engage in what you are talking about with their own ideas or further questions. This doesn't mean we will never use Yes or No or "Why" questions. It's just helpful to see the difference and try more forms of communication.

Another great tool that my wife and I have used to engage our kids in deeper conversation is to start by asking, "May I ask you a question?" This gives the other person a sense of control and can bring walls down. We found that one of our children responded especially well when asking him first if he was open to a question. He felt a sense of control and would open up more. Another way of saying this is, "I want to talk to you about something. Let me know when it's a good time to talk." I think curiosity kills them with this one. These are just a couple of things you can try that worked for my wife and me. Each child will be a little different in what they respond to best.

THE REASON BEHIND THE RESPONSE

When your child comes to a crossroad in life, where they need to make a decision about something difficult, it is going to help if they have their own conviction about it. Starting when they're young, help them engage in the reason behind the answers that you give.

For example, when our kids ask if they can watch a specific movie or TV show, saying, "That's an adult movie" might not be a satisfying answer. I hear parents say this often, and it can send a mixed message. It's important to help our kids understand that adults have the maturity required to watch different movies and shows than they watch.

When answering questions about sex, saying, "Sex in marriage is a wonderful gift," is true, but sharing why this is true, what God's intentions are for us, or what we have learned from this part of life will make a lasting impression.

How about, "I should treat every human being as if they were my brother and sister, with dignity and respect."

CHAPTER 6: WELCOME QUESTIONS

Wrestle with questions. Figure it out together. Allowing your child to be in on the process of discovering truth is a great learning process. It leads them to self-discovery and helps them take ownership of their own truth. Our behaviors come out of what we believe and the positive and negative messages that we have owned. Let your children learn and experience some answers themselves.

RESPONDING TO QUESTIONS

My son came home from grade school one day, and said "Mom and Dad, guess what a President did?" My wife and I looked at each other and paused. This was right during the President Clinton sex scandal. We were wondering how we were going to explain and thinking, *Who did he hear this from anyway? Really, are we going to be having this conversation right now?* So, we asked him what he had heard the President did? He said emphatically, "He chopped down his father's cherry tree!" We were really glad he had been learning about George Washington that day, instead of our current president, and relieved we had clarified what our son knew before we started answering a question he didn't actually ask.

This is a funny example, but the truth is, it's easy to get confused, give too much information, or even answer the entirely wrong question!

Here are some ideas for language use when talking with your kids:[103]

---

[103] Penner, C. & Penner, J. (2003). *The Gift of Sex: A Guide to Sexual Fulfillment.* Nashville, TN: W Publishing Group.

- **Affirm your child for asking.** "I'm so glad you asked." The first response is reinforcing the fact that they asked a question. This creates a feeling of safety and sends the message that it's good to ask these types of questions—making a connection. You can do this a number of ways. "Thanks for asking." "I had this same question when I was your age." "I wish I could have asked my dad this question when I was your age." "I am not sure what the answer is, but I will give it some thought and get back to you." It's more about making a connection than having the perfect answer. The fact that they asked says something. You've probably built the safety and trust we have been talking about. Typically short, concise, and age-appropriate answers are the best.

- **Repeat back to them in your own or their words, and ask if this is what they meant.** When using the skill of active listening, you are making sure you heard them correctly. You are clarifying what and how much they are really wanting to know.

- **Answer a question with a question.** "Great question. What have you heard?" "What do you think this means?" Again, this gives you more clarity to give what is needed in the moment. It's important to gain clarity about what your child is asking. Not over-answering a younger child. When you ask what they "think it means," you will sometimes learn a lot. "Well, my friend Jimmy said…"

- **Respond positively.** Respond with something positive about our human sexuality. We want our kids to connect their sexuality to God and to the gift it is to us.

CHAPTER 6: WELCOME QUESTIONS

Regardless of the question, do your best to begin with the positive before shedding light on what is or could be negative, or before giving any instructions. Share your value in a positive way without overdoing it.

- **Educate correctly.** Give them correct information. Here's what you need to know about this. Don't overcomplicate. Keep it simple.
- **Keep the dialog ongoing.** It's okay to repeat yourself. You can't count on your kids remembering what you educated them about in the third grade. You will continue to have the conversation with them throughout their growing up years and into adulthood.
- **Expect more.** Your children may ask you questions again and again. This is a good sign. It means you are a safe person to them.

AGE-APPROPRIATE TIMELINE OF TOPICS ON SEXUALITY

Keeping your responses and conversations positive is important. Some parents unintentionally provide negative, guilt-filled messages about their child's body, normal development, and sexuality.

General recommendations are to start earlier than what we once thought. In this book, I'm giving opinions based on my own parenting, interaction with other parents over the years, conventional wisdom, and a wide range of resources and voices on the topic. Check out the recommended resources in the appendix to continue exploring for yourself.

Here is a general list of topics that could be discussed and a timeline of when they might occur.

0-2 YEARS OLD

As you teach your child words, begin to teach them proper names for genitals. This helps to develop attachment, trust, and security.

2-5 YEARS OLD

Kids will have natural curiosity about their bodies. This is normal. Teach them boundaries around nudity, touching their own or other people's bodies, and privacy. Kids will begin to recognize and find interest in the differences between boys and girls. They learn to control their own body and be assertive about what they like or don't like, such as games like tickling or wrestling. They may play house or doctor with other kids or family members around their age. When this happens, redirect and discuss appropriate boundaries of their own and others' bodies in a non-shaming way. This may be a good time to discuss "tricky people" (a different word for stranger danger) and uh-oh or bad feelings.[104] Most abuse is done by people children know, so they must be made aware of having a feeling in their stomach that isn't right, stating what they are not comfortable with, even with adults, and coming to a parent when they don't feel right about something. They need language to be able to communicate these things to an adult, if needed. This is also the beginning stages of explaining reproduction.

6-9 YEARS OLD

Conversations may include technology, expectations for use, seeing nudity, and receiving or sending pictures online. Many parents will have some sort of technology contract with their children. Kids need to know the appropriate dangers of talking

---

[104] Peters, T. (2016). *Forget 'stranger danger': 'Tricky people' concept helps kids spot sketchy adults.* TODAY. Retrieved from https://www.today.com/parents/forget-stranger-danger-tricky-people-concept-helps-kids-spot-sketchy-t95021.

to strangers online and the dangers of pornography. They will be curious about how babies are made. They may need additional education on personal privacy and modesty. Creating open communication with their parents and family is important.

9-12 YEARS OLD

Kids will begin to experience puberty and become curious about the mechanics of sex. This is a great age to read a book about puberty with your child. Teach your kids about the development of the male and female body and how hormones are creating the changes they're experiencing: menstruation, wet dreams, body changes, masturbation. Body image becomes key and contributes to their level of confidence, self-esteem, insecurity, fitting in, and social acceptance. Continued conversation about pornography and messages from culture will help them during this transitional period.

TEENAGERS/YOUNG ADULT

This is a great time to focus on healthy relationships. Help them understand bonding and intimacy without being sexual, normalize sexual feelings, and learn to move from immaturity to maturity by taking responsibility for their sexual behaviors and decisions. It's imperative that they learn how to manage their sexuality as a single person. Teach them what sexual intimacy is about and what it is to have a healthy sexual relationship in marriage.

MARRIAGE

The goal isn't just to get our kids to wait for sex until marriage. It is to prepare them for a strong marriage relationship that includes:[105]

---

[105] Prepare Enrich Training.

- using good communication and conflict resolution.
- moving toward the ability to have sexual fulfillment with their spouse.
- communicating their desires and needs.
- learning how to always have respect for themselves and their partner.
- giving and receiving pleasure—allowing this to be a strong enjoyable bond in their marriage, rather than a burden.

Each family will have their own timeline, but hopefully I've given you some thoughts to explore as you develop ways to communicate with your children.

Many of the topics discussed early on will be built upon as children get older and will be adapted to each child. Firstborn children may have less and later exposure than younger children because they don't have older siblings.

Sometimes situations will influence and shift how and when we have conversations. It is easy to want to wait until later to approach the subject of sexuality.

We all wish that we didn't have to talk about puberty until our child reaches puberty or talk about relationships and sex until they're dating, but there is just too much exposure in our world for us to ignore it. Our children need to have a small part of the context before the information reaches them so they have a way to process it and know this is something they can ask questions about.

Remember, this is not about the one-time conversation, downloading everything you know in one interaction. Welcoming questions begins when they are old enough to talk and goes on throughout your relationship with your child.

CHAPTER 6
TRY THIS!

TAKE YOUR CHILD TO AN ENVIRONMENT OUTSIDE OF THE NORM AND SHARE WITH THEM YOUR PERSONAL EXPERIENCE WITH THE FOLLOWING:

1. A QUESTION WHEN YOU WERE YOUNGER THAT YOU WERE AFRAID TO ASK.

2. A TIME WHEN YOU OR SOMEONE IN YOUR FAMILY ASKED A QUESTION ABOUT SEXUALITY AND HOW IT WAS RESPONDED TO, POSITIVE OR NEGATIVE.
BE VULNERABLE.

QUESTIONS

1 | How do you think you have done so far with opening up an environment that welcomes questions?

2 | How open are you to questions from your child? What gives you this impression?

3 | Have your kids asked you a question about sexuality? If so, what was it and how did you respond?

4 | As a parent, what are some questions you are concerned your child might ask you?

CHAPTER 7

TRAIN NOT SHAME OR PUNISH

This concept is so pivotal when creating a learning environment where mistakes and struggles are allowed and become a part of the growing and maturing process. We don't punish a child as they are learning to walk—we train and instruct them. We want to take this same approach as our kids are growing into an awareness of their sexual feelings, thoughts, and behaviors.

Often, in our own decision-making, we think, *If I had known this 10 years ago, I would have done things differently.* But of course, we didn't know then, so we didn't make the decision differently. My aunt used to say, "When they knew better, they did better." When we understand something, we at least have the potential to make a better choice.

The same goes for our children. They only know what they know, and when they are born they start with knowing very little. **WE ARE NOT LOOKING TO PUNISH OUR KIDS IN THE AREA OF SEXUALITY. WE ARE STRIVING TO TEACH, TRAIN, AND GUIDE.**

TRAINING VS. PUNISHMENT

It helps if we know the difference between training and punishment. Training is connected to the student's learning, a form of teaching. Punishment is simply a negative consequence for our action. We often use the term discipline in exchange for the term punishment, but I think a better word for discipline is training. I am not suggesting that natural consequences for our children's actions are wrong or bad. Their behaviors may include consequences. I am suggesting, however, that the primary focus should be on helping our kids learn, not just making them feel bad by our words or by the outcome. If we focus on punishment only, we miss the bigger picture of training and guiding. From a teaching perspective, learning happens when the student gets it, when the light turns on, or when insight is gained. Learning doesn't just happen when the instructor gives out the information.

If we think of our American prison system, one of the big arguments is whether we should have punitive or restorative justice. Dr. Fania Davis makes a clarifying statement about this: "Punitive justice asks only what rule or law was broken, who did it, and how they should be punished. It responds to the original harm with more harm. Restorative justice asks who was harmed, what are the needs and obligations of all affected, and how do they figure out how to heal the harm."[106]

THE BIGGER PICTURE: WE WANT OUR HOMES TO BE A PLACE OF INSTRUCTION—A PLACE OF ENDEARMENT.

We wouldn't want our children to think of home as a prison where they are just waiting until they get out on parole. If you've

---

[106] Davis, F. (2014). *Discipline With Dignity: Oakland Classrooms Try Healing Instead of Punishment*. Retrieved from https://www.yesmagazine.org/issues/education-uprising/where-dignity-is-part-of-the-school-day.

CHAPTER 7: TRAIN NOT SHAME OR PUNISH

ever been grounded, like I have, maybe you've entertained this thought.

What does a home or a parent-child relationship that is restorative look like? How do we get there? What did our upbringing teach us? Was our upbringing more training or shaming? What does it look like when we miss it and focus only on the punishment? And, how do we change our paradigm if what we were modeled was more punishment focused and our heart is to train and guide our children—to do it differently?

Let me tell you a story about one of my early memories. In the early 70s, when I was six or seven years old, growing up in California, it was a hot summer day and a neighborhood friend, a couple of years older, dared my brother and me to take off our shorts and go streaking through the neighborhood. My brother and I did exactly what he said. Dumb went first and dumber followed him.

While we are running up and down the street naked, a neighbor saw us and called my mom to let her know. My brother and I were sent to our rooms to wait until our dad came home. When Dad got home, he started in my brother's room. I could hear him scolding my brother for what we did and then spanking him bare-bottomed, and I remember hearing my brother loudly crying. As a little boy, I realized that my turn was next, and even thought about crawling out the window because "all hell was about to break loose." When my dad came into my room, the same thing happened to me. Through my tears and pain I perceived he wasn't *for me*. I was pretty young and just trying to be silly and have fun. I was treated like I did something very bad. This was the perception from my young mind. In this situation, what my brother and I needed wasn't to be punished. We needed to be trained and guided.

CONVERSATION

My dad did the best he knew at the time. He was part of a culture that believed punishment was the answer. Looking back, I see the message that was communicated to me as a young kid and know it wasn't helpful. When my dad walked out of the room, one of my thoughts was, *He's not safe. Whatever I do, don't ever let him catch me doing something wrong.* It made me want to hide, to stay disconnected.

The goal is to keep connection with our children as much as possible, even in situations that call for consequences.

I know there were times, in my own parenting, that I reacted from my upbringing and used punishment, even though it wasn't my intention either. I believe each generation has to build on the last and hopefully learn and improve.

A PART OF OUR PERSONAL HEALTH IS TO BE ABLE TO LOOK AT WHAT WE WERE HANDED AND GROW FROM IT. If there is healing to be done or forgiveness to be extended, then the work of this will free us up to build on what we were given.

Today my dad is one of my best friends. He showed his love to me in many ways throughout my childhood and taught me a lot of valuable things. However, I needed to sort through the messages I perceived, whether they were intentional or not, to be able to heal from them and not operate out of those wounds anymore.

I want to take a closer look at this story and help us learn from it. There are several principles I see in this that are valuable in training our kids. First of all, stay connected and don't create a sense of isolation between you and your child—to respond rather than react, guide them, allow natural consequences using boundaries, know the difference, and choose an approach that is not shaming.

CHAPTER 7: TRAIN NOT SHAME OR PUNISH

CONNECTION

In response to my streaking adventure, it would have been more helpful for my brother and me to have a conversation with Mom or Dad (or both) about when nudity is and is not appropriate, such as in the shower or the bathroom, and not in public. Or to be taught that just because someone older than us tells us to do something, we don't have to do it. Sending me to my room to think about my behavior and wait for Dad to deal with me, creates a sense of separation and isolation. Unfortunately, this used to be a common practice, using isolation as a form of punishment. I believe parents didn't always know what else to do.

RESPOND VS. REACT

My dad responded out of what I presumed to be anger, frustration, and his own embarrassment. As a parent, it is valuable to be aware of our own emotions—to step back and evaluate what would be the best response to the specific situation. This is an example of being punished instead of trained.

My dad's message to me was that my behavior was very bad, but as a young child, I heard it as a shame message: I am bad. He was speaking about the behavior, but I took it as a value statement. The scolding and spanking I received said to me, "What I did was very bad, don't ever do this again." Our children don't have all of the reasoning process to figure out what's happening.

In my streaking story, I think this is a pretty common occurrence for some parents—reacting out of personal embarrassment or anger. I've done this myself. I may not know what to do or how to handle the situation. Many times discipline comes as an overreaction to our children's behavior, not as a response. We think, *When my child misbehaves, what does this say about me?* Our false beliefs tell us, *I'm not a good parent,* or *My child is disrespecting me, so I am doing something wrong.* What is the best approach?

As parents, we need to allow our souls to heal so we no longer carry shame. We can use the tool we discussed earlier, IFAB: "**I feel** embarrassed **about** my child streaking through the neighborhood, **because** I believe it reflects that I'm a bad parent."

Take the opportunity to slow down: "...be quick to listen, slow to speak and slow to become angry."[107] **A delayed response is often better than a quick overreaction.** We need to remind ourselves, *I don't have to take care of this right now.* Not every moment is the training moment. We might wait a few hours or even the next day. As parents, there is value in stopping, observing what we're feeling, and asking ourselves: *What is it that I want to teach my child through this situation and how can I best communicate this to them?*

We don't want to be parents who use idle threats either. "You're grounded today, grounded all summer, grounded the rest of your life!" This just separates us from the heart of our child and from our real goal of correcting while still maintaining connection.[108] Sometimes we misrepresent our true heart toward our children.

It is easy to have a relationship with our child's behavior rather than connecting to their heart and what's underneath the behavior.

AS PARENTS, WE NEED TO TRY TO UNDERSTAND OUR KIDS' PERSPECTIVES—TO BE THE SAFEST PEOPLE WE CAN BE FOR THEM.

Fear-based approaches can sometimes be effective. This can facilitate an immediate result, but more often than not, it can be harmful in the long run. There is much more awareness of this

---

[107] James 1:19

[108] Purvis, K., Cross, D., Dansereau, D., & Parris, S. (2013). Trust-based relational intervention (TBRI®): A systematic approach to complex developmental trauma. *Child & Youth Services, 34*(4), 360-386.

CHAPTER 7: TRAIN NOT SHAME OR PUNISH

now, and in schools and homes parents are often used to different approaches that are less fear-based. This is truly a step forward.

PG: PARENTAL GUIDANCE SUGGESTED

It is normal for kids to be curious. They don't come with automatic knowledge in any area of their lives, including sexuality, so they are going to need someone to guide them. If we expect this will happen—that our kids will need continuous guidance—we will be less likely to overreact when their curiosity gets the best of them. Curiosity can come in many forms: nudity (as in the story I shared), touching themselves, mimicking what they see others do, or even an attraction to something harmful, such as pornography or something they see online.

If we are expecting this, we won't be shocked or angry and will be ready to respond with an attitude of teaching and training rather than punishing. Our approach could be, "My kids are developing an understanding about their human sexuality, and it's my responsibility to guide them. I see this as a guiding moment." This is a better approach than experiencing embarrassment or giving a quick response, giving them the impression they've done something wrong. If we have taught them this before, and they are choosing to do something they know is wrong or disobedient, we are still guiding them through the situation with age-appropriate instruction and appropriate consequences.

One of my sons once mimicked his grade school friend on the bus doing something inappropriate. His teacher contacted me and explained the situation. I said something like this, "Thank you for bringing this to my attention. I will talk to my son about it. He is still learning, and I want to guide him and help him understand why this behavior isn't appropriate." My natural emotional response would be to overreact to the situation. This time I chose to slow down, listen first, and choose what I felt was the best response for the situation. I didn't want to overreact to the teacher, in defense of my son or because of my own embarrassment, but my biggest desire was to make this a learning experience for my child. I was able to have a conversation with my son to gain clarity about what happened and how it happened. He explained the situation and that he was mimicking a friend on the school bus. This was a great opportunity to teach my son how to respond rather than react himself. When we slow down, we are able to check in with our internal voice before making a decision. In this situation with my son, the natural consequence was to follow up with the teacher or others involved and make amends. As a father, I didn't choose to shame or punish my son. I did choose to allow the natural consequence to be a teacher.

There are many instances where I didn't get it "all right," but fortunately, this wasn't the only time I chose to train and guide, instead of shame and punish. I remember distinctly other times I chose to instruct rather than punish my kids—like the time my son's gratitude was evident by his response in throwing his arms around me with tears in his eyes and saying, "Thank you, Dad. I love you." He didn't feel shamed or that he was in trouble. I had educated myself and was intentional about offering him grace and truth.

Your child may be the older sibling in your home, but that won't be true of all of their classmates or young friends. They may overhear things that are said or something on television and repeat it. Some parents will be shocked or upset, without clarifying where the child heard this from and if they even know what it means.

When my wife's sister was in grade school she went to a slumber party with other girls from church and told them a joke about parents having sex. The adults who heard about it were upset and called her parents. She was pretty young and didn't actually know what the joke meant or much about sex. Rather than being punished, it was an opportunity to talk to her about the meaning of what she said and why it was inappropriate to share with others.

Even as kids get older, they certainly don't have the full picture of sexuality and the appropriate ways to manage it. This is part of our role in guiding and teaching them. **ALL OF US ARE STILL LEARNING AS WE MOVE INTO ADULTHOOD AND DEVELOP INTIMATE RELATIONSHIPS, BOTH SEXUAL AND NONSEXUAL.**

Obviously, we will use discernment as to what the appropriate follow-up is for our child in each individual situation. Our actions sometimes require natural or intentional consequences. There may be times when our child's behavior is more serious and we need to address it as such. If we aren't prepared, we might feel embarrassed by what others will think and respond poorly to our kids. We need to use discernment in this so even consequences stay instructive. We may want to step back and ask ourselves, *What is the message I want to send to my child when I address this situation?*

We need to remember our overall goal and how to best achieve this goal.

NATURAL CONSEQUENCES

Natural consequences are a central way we learn. If we touch a hot stove, we will get burned. We set appropriate boundaries to keep ourselves and our kids safe. This same rule applies to other behaviors as well. Love is not boundaryless. We follow through with the consequences when the boundaries are crossed.

It's important that we don't step in and rescue our child from the natural consequence. Many consequences big and small can be a powerful teacher. Stepping in is natural for many parents, but it can often be enabling and create a sense of entitlement. When we don't allow ourselves or others to experience natural consequences it can keep all of us from learning and maturing. **GROWING COMES FROM FACING AND WORKING THROUGH DIFFICULTIES AND EXPERIENCING THE CONSEQUENCES OF OUR CHOICES.** When we teach our children the potential consequence behind a decision, we are much further along in helping them make the decision for themselves. When our kids are young, we typically make decisions for them, like keeping them from running into the street; but as they grow, they will need to understand the reason behind the choice and choose it for themselves when we are not around. They need to be able to make important decisions when they come to a crossroads in their life.

I remember a time when one of my sons was caught lying. I said to him, "I know where you get lying from—it comes from your mother's side of the family." No, I didn't say this. I actually said, "Your dad has lied before, and I realized it's not the better way. It can be really convenient sometimes. Telling the truth can be hard, but lying has consequences," and I pointed out that the local jail has a lot of people in it who have lied and are living with the effects of their choices. I continued to say, "You have a decision to make. You can lie to yourself, to your boss, to your spouse someday. You can grow up lying if you want. You get to be a liar or a truthteller. I want you to think about this. I have chosen in my life to be a truthteller." I wanted my son to see the reasons behind why we make decisions, as well as the consequences of our choices.

CHAPTER 7: TRAIN NOT SHAME OR PUNISH

Even though our kids may experience consequences, either natural or intentional, the main goal is training—helping them learn through experience.

Natural consequences mean that we allow our kids to learn from their choices. We have to ask ourselves, *What is the lesson to be learned in this situation?* As a parent, are we taking time to train our children or shaming them? This may take a process of retraining ourselves for this to come naturally, but we can all learn by being intentional.

It really comes down to a lot of conversations—not yelling or scolding—and learning how to listen and respond rather than react. Also, not using absolute words like *always* and *never*.

It may seem like we're having the same conversations over and over again, but this is part of parenting—part of helping our children understand and grow. The bottom line: conversation, conversation, conversation.

IT'S IMPORTANT TO RECOGNIZE WHEN OUR PARENTING IS SHAMING AND WHEN IT'S TRAINING TOWARD OUR KIDS. Here are a few common situations and examples of natural consequences:

SITUATION: NOT COMPLETING CHORES WHEN ASKED

NATURAL CONSEQUENCE
Embarrassment from dirty clothes or a messy house, financial cost of replacement if lost or broken (phone is left under a pile of dirty laundry on the floor and stepped on), etc.

SHAMING/PUNISHING REACTION
- Your room looks like a pig's pen. (degrading)
- You *never* do what I ask you to do. (absolute words)
- You *never* get your chores done when I ask.

TRAINING RESPONSE
- When you get your chores done, you can...watch TV, play outside, have dessert.

(Setting up positive results on the front end and then following through with the expectation.)

SITUATION: DISRESPECTFUL TOWARD A PARENT

NATURAL CONSEQUENCE
Negative impact on relationship, influence on siblings, etc.

SHAMING/PUNISHING REACTION
- You're *always* disrespectful to us. (absolute words)
- You can't talk to me this way! You're grounded!
- Yelling at our kids and sending them to their room.

TRAINING RESPONSE
- When you talk to me this way, it makes me feel...
- You have been talking disrespectful to me lately and I want you to know it hurts me when you talk to me this way.
- I am trying to be respectful in my communication with you. I would like for you to be respectful when you communicate with me.

CHAPTER 7: TRAIN NOT SHAME OR PUNISH

SITUATION: DRUG/ALCOHOL USE

NATURAL CONSEQUENCE
Legal issues (MIP, DUI, DWI), suspended drivers license, increased insurance rates, school suspension, health impact, etc.

SHAMING/PUNISHING REACTION
- Don't ever let me catch you doing this again!
- If I ever find out you've used drugs or alcohol, you'll be in so much trouble! (empty threat)

TRAINING RESPONSE
- Here are some of the problems I have seen associated with drug and alcohol use when I was growing up.
- If you are in a situation where there are drugs and alcohol, you can always call me and I will come get you.
- I want to be a safe person for you to talk with about this, whether before, during, or after you make a choice.
- Let's talk about the environments and relationships you are in and what boundaries to put around them.

SITUATION: INAPPROPRIATE MESSAGE/IMAGE ON PHONE

NATURAL CONSEQUENCE
Embarrassment, forwarded to another person, potential legal consequences, etc.

SHAMING/PUNISHING REACTION
- I can't believe you would do something like this. We taught you better.
- What were you thinking?
- You embarrassed our family.

- You're not going to be able to have social media any more because you can't handle it.

TRAINING RESPONSE
Sit down and talk about what's going on with them.
- What did this mean to you?
- What message were you trying to get across?
- How do you think you could make this right?
- What steps could you take to make this right?
- What do you think we need to do to monitor your phone use going forward?

(Together, coming up with a plan to help them.)

SITUATION: FAILING GRADE IN A CLASS

NATURAL CONSEQUENCE
Cannot participate in school sports, retake the class, summer school, detention, etc.

SHAMING/PUNISHING REACTION
- You're lazy!
- We've done so much for you, and you don't make any effort.
- You're grounded for the whole summer!
- You're not going to do anything until all of your grades are As.

TRAINING RESPONSE
- How can I help you to get your homework completed so you are able to play sports next season?
- What do you think the struggle is with your grades?

- How do you feel about your effort in your classes?
- What support do you need to get your makeup work done and participate in future activities?
- What do you think is a good boundary to help you keep up with your schoolwork?

Sometimes we react (or overreact) to our children because we feel unprepared and overwhelmed. We may be dealing with any number of our own issues, as well as trying to help our children. Again, I would suggest that you seek out support. Don't try to do this alone.

This is an opportunity to grow and not shame or punish ourselves as well. How are you doing with this? As parents, we are in training too.

GUILT VS. SHAME

Many times guilt and shame get lumped into the same category. We think of guilt as a bad thing. Guilt can actually be constructive when it's not tied to shame. Shame is about our identity: "I am bad." Guilt, when used the right way, says, "I did something bad."[109] It can be our conscience telling us we're headed down a road that is not going to be beneficial. Guilt may produce negative feelings, such as regret, sadness, anxiety, or fear. These are feelings, not beliefs about myself. Shame is more than a feeling, although shame can carry very negative feelings as well. Shame is about the nature of who we are and our core beliefs.

---

[109] Brown, B. (2015). *Daring Greatly: How the Courage to Be Vulnerable Transforms the Way We Live, Love, Parent, and Lead.* New York, NY: Penguin Random House.

SHAME DRIVES US TO ISOLATION AND CREATES AN ATMOSPHERE OF KEEPING SECRETS, FEARING PUNISHMENT OR CONSEQUENCES. Shame is at the root of so much of our dysfunction. As parents, if we have dealt with our own shame, and are letting our children see that we are growing through our mistakes and working on letting go of our own shame, we can help them do the same.

Some of us grew up hearing people say, "Shame on you," in response to someone's decision. I have a friend who says it this way: "Shame off you."

Author and shame researcher, Brene Brown, talks about building shame resilience. "Even though we can't eliminate shame, we can become more resilient to it."[110] She calls it "that ability to recognize shame when we experience it, and move through it in a constructive way that allows us to maintain our authenticity and grow from our experiences."[111] To move through shame, we must recognize it, know we are not alone, reach out—the single most powerful act of resilience—and speak out our shame. Shame is most harmful when it goes unacknowledged and is not spoken of with others. If we don't know how to process our problems and pain, they become unresolved issues of loss and don't go away on their own.

THREE BIBLICAL EXAMPLES

If Jesus was walking through our world today, how would He interact with people who have struggled with their sexuality—whether the teenager trapped in pornography, the spouse who is unfaithful to their partner, the registered sex offender (who is

---

[110] Ibid.

[111] Ibid.

CHAPTER 7: TRAIN NOT SHAME OR PUNISH

often an abused child who becomes the abuser), or the person who is confused about their sexuality?

I'm grateful we have examples of how Jesus interacted with sexually broken people in His day. This gives us insight into God's heart to restore and heal. Remember, Jesus came to show us what God (Father, Son, and Holy Spirit) is like.

Scripture tells a story of Jesus meeting a Samaritan woman. This is one of my favorite stories in Scripture because Jesus seems to do so many things that were culturally taboo. There were religious differences, societal barriers, and gender issues that would have kept Jesus and this woman from meeting, let alone having conversation.[112] I love this text because it shows God's heart—that all people matter!

Jesus asked her a question and engaged her in conversation. In this conversation, He addresses that she's been married five times and the person she is now with is not her husband. She confirms this was true. Whether she had sexual or relationship addictions, or had been wounded in her past and thought her worth was tied to her sexuality, she was clearly broken and searching for something.

After her conversation with Jesus, she leaves and goes back to town and says to the people, "Come, see a man who told me everything I ever did. Could this be the Messiah?"[113] I've never had anyone say, "Someone knows all my negative sexual history—you've got to meet this guy! Maybe he knows yours too!" Somehow she was not put off by Jesus addressing her mistakes. From her perspective, He must have been someone who offered hope not condemnation. She believed Him when He said He was offering "living water."

---

[112] Cavey, B. (2007). *The End of Religion: Encountering the Subversive Spirituality of Jesus.* Colorado Springs, CO: NavPress.

[113] John 4:29

Her encounter with Jesus was so impactful that Church history knows (records) her as St. Photina and believes her to be the first missionary to the Samaritan people.[114] She and her sons suffered and died a martyr's death for not renouncing their faith in Christ.

There is also a story of a man who could have been healed from his brokenness, but he didn't show up to the meeting, so they just brought the woman. Scripture titles this "The Woman Caught in Adultery." I like to call it, "The Man Who Missed His Opportunity." He missed his opportunity for healing.

The woman wasn't found alone. Scripture actually says she was caught during the act—clearly there were two people involved. While Jesus is teaching, the religious leaders bring just the woman to Jesus. They were trying to trap Jesus and their motive wasn't restoration for these two people. Had the Pharisees brought both of them to Jesus, I'm sure He would have offered hope and healing for the man as well.

The Pharisees said to Jesus, "The law of Moses says to stone her, but what do you say?"[115] Jesus knelt in the sand and wrote something, and the woman's accusers began to leave one by one, until only Jesus and her were left. Jesus stood and asked her, "Woman, where are those who condemn you?"[116] "They are gone," she said. "Neither do I condemn you," Jesus declared. "Now go and sin no more."[117]

---

[114] The Orthodox Church in America (2019). Martyr Photina the Samaritan Woman, her sons, and those with them. Retrieved from https://www.oca.org/saints/lives/2020/03/20/100846-martyr-photina-the-samaritan-woman-her-sons-and-those-with-them.

[115] John 8:5

[116] John 8:10

[117] John 8:11

CHAPTER 7: TRAIN NOT SHAME OR PUNISH

A third, and equally impactful story, is about a woman who Scripture says was openly living a sinful life, yet she felt safe enough to approach Jesus in an extremely vulnerable way, in front of and in the home of a judgmental religious person.

Jesus was having dinner at the home of a Pharisee—not always the most accepting group of people. The woman, who was presumed a prostitute, washed Jesus' feet with her tears, wiped them with her hair, kissed His feet, and poured perfume on Him in an act of gratitude.[118] The religious people saw this and scolded Jesus. "If this man were a prophet, he would know who is touching him and what kind of a woman she is—that she is a sinner."[119] Jesus calls them out on missing the point and raises the woman's worth and dignity in front of them. The Pharisee missed what Christ is all about, and the woman recognized it.

In these three stories, Jesus wasn't trying to shame or punish anyone. When we have missed the mark in managing our sexuality, it doesn't change God's heart to help and heal us.

I think this is really important. I looked at how Christ dealt with sexual brokenness and how Jesus treated people who, in His culture, were struggling or broken. I saw an individual who wasn't condemning or shaming, but who was elevating people where they were at and offering hope, redemption, and a better way.

A HEALTHY VIEW OF GOD IS TO SEE HIM AS SOMEONE WHO HAS NOTHING BUT OUR BEST INTEREST IN MIND. I now see Jesus as a reflection of the heart of God, who came not to point an accusing finger (shaming), but to extend His hand (to help).[120]

---

[118] Luke 7:38

[119] Luke 7:39

[120] John 3:17

CHAPTER 7
TRY THIS!

THIS WEEK, CATCH EACH PERSON IN YOUR FAMILY "DOING SOMETHING RIGHT" AND LET THEM KNOW YOU NOTICED.

OR

TALK TO YOUR SPOUSE OR A TRUSTED FRIEND ABOUT A TIME IN YOUR LIFE WHERE YOU FELT SHAMED, NOT TRAINED OR GUIDED.

QUESTIONS

1 | How do you recognize the difference between training and punishment?

2 | Can you identify an area in your life where you want to work on your own shame?

3 | Think of a time when you reacted rather than responded? How would you like to have done things differently?

4 | From the three Scriptures where Jesus interacts with sexually broken people, what are some personal observations?

CHAPTER 8

FOCUS ON GROWTH NOT PERFECTION

WE KNOW WHAT WE KNOW

A young boy asked his father, "Dad, do you think Jesus ever made mistakes?"[121] What a great question for a child to ask his dad. The father paused, thinking about the answer to this for himself, and replied with a question, "What do you think?" The kid thought for a moment, then said, "Well, if he didn't make mistakes, how would he have learned anything?"

Jesus grew in wisdom and stature…[122]

Is it just part of being human to make mistakes? **Don't confuse making a mistake with sinning.** Making a mistake isn't always sinful. How did Jesus learn? Do you think that He ever made mistakes? Do you think that when He learned to speak He already knew Aramaic? Do you think when He learned to walk, He never fell down? Did He get to skip potty training? When He built His first table with His father in the carpenter shop, was it perfectly level? Did He ever make mistakes? Maybe this is where the construction saying comes from: *measure twice, cut once.* Could

---

[121] Author Paul Young shared this story in a conference I attended.

[122] Luke 2:52

this have come from Joseph teaching Jesus about carpentry? We do know that Jesus was fully God and yet fully human.

The truth is, we don't come into this world knowing much of anything. ==SO MUCH OF LIFE IS ABOUT GOING FROM IMMATURITY TO MATURITY. OUR LEARNING COMES THROUGH TRAINING AND EXPERIENCES.==

I remember a time in grade school, at my private school in sunny California, leaning up against a tree, having lunch with my buddies. Somehow we got to the subject of sex, and one of my friends took the honor of sharing with us some details of the act of sex. He concluded by saying, "Your mom and dad do this. That's how you got here." My other friend said, "Not my mom and dad, they're Christians." They both looked at me, and I said, "Not mine. Mine are pastors." I look back at this conversation and just laugh—these three little monkeys sitting under a tree, trying to figure out the world and how it all works. We obviously still had some learning and growing to do.

ENVIRONMENTS OF GROWTH— GROWING TOGETHER

> ANYONE WHO HAS NEVER MADE A MISTAKE HAS NEVER TRIED ANYTHING NEW.[123]

Environments of growth are so beneficial in all areas of life and definitely in the area of healthy sexuality. We might not have all the resources we need to help our kids, but we must be willing to lead them to people and tools that can help them when they need it.

---

[123] BrainyQuote (2019). Albert Einstein quote. Retrieved from https://www.brainyquote.com/quotes/albert_einstein_109012.

CHAPTER 8: FOCUS ON GROWTH NOT PERFECTION

The fact that you are taking the time to read this book, shows your commitment to growth.

The brain develops by observing.[124]

Your children will observe how you respond to your own mistakes, their mistakes, and the mistakes of others. They will see what you "believe about making mistakes."

I believe in my children, that they will make good decisions, but they know I don't expect they will make every decision correctly. This just wouldn't be possible. They know that when they make a mistake, they are going to process it and look at how they think and feel about it. I actually do this with them; and now that my children are adults, I am available to help them process their mistakes, as well as talk about my own mistakes and process how I am growing.

If you still see yourself as growing, you will have an easier time seeing this as an option for your kids and your kids will see this in you too.

My father is in his 90s now and I have seen him continue to grow as a parent, in his relationship with my mom, and in his understanding about life and God. This has continued to increase my respect for him and given me permission to keep growing myself. Who knew, when I thought my dad was perfect, that he would actually model more by his ability to grow than by my perception of him getting it right all the time.

---

[124] Little, B. (2014). Mindfulness and Mirror Neurons in Learning. MindTools. Retrieved from https://www.mindtools.com/blog/corporate/mindfulness-and-mirror-neurons-in-learning/.

PERFECTIONISM

The practice of mindfulness is so common now.[125] It is something most of us are familiar with. Most kids are learning about it in school. To learn nonjudgmental acceptance instead of the expectation of perfection is a gift. To be mindful means to be present, but it is also means to observe—to be curious rather than critical of yourself and others. We must start with accepting all parts of ourselves.[126] If we grow up thinking the point is to be good, do it right, and never make mistakes, we will not embrace the way we are designed—to come into this world knowing very little, but learn and grow.

In my home, my family has adopted many self-care practices that are beneficial and contribute to focusing and being in the moment. Some of these practices include: deep breathing; focusing on one thing at a time, whether it is eating or driving; doing something with another family member; meditation (slowing down the mind to listen to the Spirit); or exercise. Yes, even Sudoku puzzles. This really builds our "brain muscle" to be able to practice being present, which can contribute to the nonjudgmental acceptance of ourselves and others.

As parents, we, of course, want good things for our children. We want them to have successes and wins in their lives. The danger is when we are afraid of failure, and repeatedly shield them from the natural learning process that comes from looking at life's experiences as growing opportunities. Rigid, rule-based homes sometimes produce standards that are simply too hard for our kids to live up to. On the opposite end, chaotic homes

---

[125] Ibid.

[126] Riemersma, J. (2019). Pastoral Sex Addiction Professional (PSAP) Training. International Institute for Trauma & Addiction Professionals. February.

CHAPTER 8: FOCUS ON GROWTH NOT PERFECTION

are not healthy either. There is a way to accept and grow with appropriate structure and boundaries.

This is something we learn when we want to be a parent who is full of grace and truth.[127] **GRACE ALLOWS MISTAKES AND TRUTH ALLOWS HONESTY AND NATURAL CONSEQUENCES.** It can be a challenge to allow our children to have natural consequences for their actions. It can be equally challenging to extend grace when they are pushing our buttons. As parents, sometimes when we follow through with consequences, it punishes us too, canceling individual or family plans, or perhaps creating extra work for us.

I have witnessed many parents who swoop in and try to fix the problems for their kids, not allowing their child to fail. Sometimes this comes from a codependent rescuing behavior. Often, it comes from fear. We may fear for our child's wellbeing or even their life, in some cases, or we may fear we will lose relationship with them. We may fear what others will think of our family, our child, or our parenting. It takes a lot of health to discern what is in the best interest of our child and to set aside some of the natural, but more unhealthy motives.

It becomes easier if we understand about resilience. Facing fears and problems is what brings growth. **Resilience is a very important part of our children's growth and development.** If they aren't allowed to fail, it is hard to build resilience. We want our children to be in an environment where they aren't afraid of failure. Do our kids believe the goal is to do everything right? We might want to ask them.

We can tell our kids that it's okay to make mistakes, but they are watching whether this is experientially true. In other words,

---
[127] John 1:14; John 1:17

our logical brain can tell us one thing while our emotional brain tells us another. This is why it is so important that experience backs up our thinking. Do they see that we're okay with our own imperfections and mistakes? How do they see us respond or talk about others and their mistakes? Our kids must see that we actually believe mistakes are okay, whether it is ourselves, them, or others who make the mistake. Out of this comes our actual belief system. This is one way we know that a person's actions are more impactful than their words.

One of the best ways to let go of perfection is to learn to laugh at ourselves. Not all situations are a laughing matter, but many are. Some situations we may laugh about later. If we see the humor in being human, our children will learn this to some extent as well. There are many things that happen that are very serious. Learn to discern which can be classified as, "don't sweat the small stuff" and celebrated as part of life.[128] Anyone with grown kids knows that there is a bit of a sibling code sometimes, for crazy things they do that they don't tell parents until later. Some things, like driving your dad's motorhome to school at 16 years old, aren't funny until later.[129]

ASKING FOR HELP

In the area of sexuality, an important part of training our kids is making sure they know they can ask for help. If they've learned they're not expected to know all of the answers and that mistakes are part of learning, they're going to believe it's okay to ask for help—whether before, during, or after a situation.

---

[128] Carlson, R. (1997). *Don't Sweat the Small Stuff...and It's All Small Stuff: Simple Ways to Keep the Little Things from Taking Over Your Life.* New York, NY: Hyperion.

[129] I can neither confirm, nor deny, this happened.

CHAPTER 8: FOCUS ON GROWTH NOT PERFECTION

This was something I really wanted my children to understand. I realized that if they were punished every time they came to me, they would stop coming to me. I even experienced this sometimes. It became important that we looked at consequences together and we explored how we would grow from a situation. This changed our relationship. When my kids made a choice they didn't feel good about, or even if their friends made a poor choice, they felt open to come to me and share it. I felt this gave me a much bigger window into their world than if I was just trying to find the appropriate punishment for mistakes they made.

GRACE FOR THE GROWNUPS

How are you doing with allowing yourself to not be perfect? Do you beat yourself up when you make mistakes or are you embracing growth in yourself? If you thought the point was to be the "perfect parent," you might have quickly discovered it isn't so easy.

I often laugh at the pre-parent or new parent who watches everyone else—their siblings and friends—and says, "When I'm a parent, I will never allow that!" What works for one child doesn't work for every child. God bless those who birthed all easy, compliant children; but most of us discovered early on that there wasn't a one-size-fits-all manual for each child and each growth stage. We bounced along making mistakes.

I'm here to tell you to have so much grace for yourself. Life will give you many opportunities to grow, like it or not. If you want to change your attitude about it right now, you have permission to do so.

My wife and I have so many examples of making mistakes as humans and as parents, so we are right there with you. We have many examples of ways that we have missed it and what we learned from our experiences.

One of my children, who I will lovingly refer to as "strong-willed," kept my wife and me on our toes. Fortunately, he had a strong moral compass, but when it came to challenging us, he was 100 percent up for the task, pretty much from the age of two on. One time when he was barely old enough to have a full conversation, he was reprimanded for disobeying, and was angry at my wife. He said, "Just wait until I tell Dad when he gets home." In all fairness, he was our most sentimental and tender child, he just felt very deeply and still does to this day. Later in his teenager years, when we went through some counseling to help us resolve conflict with him, we would often come home and try out the tools we had learned. Sometimes, when something worked, it seemed like magic. Afterwards, my wife and I would go up to the master bedroom, lock the door, and high five each other. "Yay! Something actually worked."

Other times it seemed like a train wreck. My wife and I would lock the door and stare at each other or say, "What are we doing wrong?" One time my wife told me, "Today, I was so discouraged. I started to beat myself up over and over again: *We suck as parents!*" She continued, "I stopped myself and said, 'No we don't. There's a lot worse we could have done. We're normal parents. We are just doing the best job we can.'" This wasn't our first experience with feeling this way and it wasn't the last.

I've heard moms say that their teenagers helped them understand why some animals eat their young. If you feel strong emotions around being a parent sometimes, we're right there with you. All of us have experienced both the highs of feeling we did a great job and the lows of thinking, *Just about anybody could have handled this situation better than I did.*

There have been times in raising my kids where you might look at me and say, "Rodney, you have amazing kids. You should

CHAPTER 8: FOCUS ON GROWTH NOT PERFECTION

write a book." There are other times where you might say to me, "Rodney, you're missing it. You should buy a book."

Sometimes we react automatically, and we didn't expect it. Sometimes we call this "going limbic."[130] In the moment, instead of making the logical response we would usually make, or the one we would like to make, our brain goes into a fight, flight, or freeze pattern and we respond emotionally.

My wife experienced this recently. She was out to dinner with our daughter Whitney, and Whitney locked the keys in the car. This normally wouldn't have been a big deal, but I was out of town, and my wife felt a little panicked and overreacted. Afterward, my wife felt like her reaction was shaming toward our daughter. She didn't regulate her emotions on the inside and it came out as an overreaction. She immediately felt bad about it and apologized.

Several months later, the day before Whitney's wedding, my wife was busy getting things ready and setting up the reception. Her emotions were pretty high on the inside. Whitney was carrying a large drink server out to the car and dropped and broke the top of it. They both looked at each other, knowing this was "another wedding expense" and not much time to replace it. This time, my wife was able to stop and respond differently. She had stored the memory of her previous response and how it felt to overreact. My wife said, "It's okay. It's not a big deal. We'll find another one or make do." She laughed about it and said, "If this is the worst thing that happens, it's going to be a great wedding!" Even though she had some of the same emotions on the inside—anxious and not sure what to do

---

[130] Roberts, T. (2014). *Seven Pillars of Freedom Workbook*. Gresham, OR: Pure Desire Ministries International.

next—she was able to handle the situation differently and put herself and Whitney at ease. Later that day, Whitney came up to her, hugged her, and spontaneously said, "I love you, Mom." My wife described this outcome as worth any broken object. She wouldn't have traded this experience of connection and acceptance with our daughter for anything.

We may react out of a lack of acceptance of ourselves and this comes out on others. **WHEN WE EXPERIENCE STRONG EMOTIONS, THEY AREN'T NECESSARILY TIED TO THE CURRENT EXPERIENCE.** A great tool to evaluate an over- or under-reaction in yourself is called a Road to the Wound. This is included in the appendix. It is a tool that helps us make a connection to our automatic responses that sometimes aren't tied to the current event or situation. In other words, it looks at what "pushes our buttons." Our response is often tied to the message or "false belief" that is triggered by the experience. This is why doing our own personal work and *Pursuing Personal Health* (chapter 1) spills out onto those around us and often those we love most. Road to the Wound is a great tool to process with a spouse, friend, family, or in a small group.

A big part of focusing on growth is about modeling to our kids by taking responsibility, owning our actions, and learning to make amends. Keep growing!

HONESTY AND SAFETY

One of the best ways we grow is in an honest environment. In fact, I would say that it is very difficult to grow if we aren't honest, and we usually won't be honest if we don't feel safe. Our children are watching from the beginning and seeing if we

CHAPTER 8: FOCUS ON GROWTH NOT PERFECTION

are safe people in many different ways. How we do anything is how we do everything.[131]

Are we judgmental of others? Are we judgmental of ourselves? Do we teach our kids by our words or actions that God is judgmental? Do we assume that all humans need help growing or do we judge others by the mistakes they make? All of this will shape our kids' perception of us and whether we are safe. This will dictate how safe it is to be honest with us.

For example, you see a friend's child make a mistake. You could say, "The Wright's aren't good parents. Look at the mistakes their child is making," making a judgment on the family in front of your kids or you could respond differently. You could say, "The Wright's child made a mistake. This could be a great learning opportunity. I've made mistakes as well, both as a parent and as a child." How you respond to the mistakes of others sends a loud message to your child as to how you might respond to their mistakes when they happen.

WE WANT TO TEACH OUR CHILDREN THAT MISTAKES ARE TO BE EXPECTED, EMBRACED, AND A PART OF LIFE.

When our kids are learning to walk and they fall, we don't say, "Take this one back, they're defective. They can't even walk. Give me one that doesn't fall, please." Falling is a part of the process of learning how to walk. We will stumble along the way. Again, we want to create an environment of growth, not performance.

An important part of growth and development is to normalize and validate our children's thoughts, feelings, and experiences.[132]

---

[131] Rohr, R. (2004). *Adam's Return: The Five Promises of Male Initiation.* New York, NY: The Crossroad Publishing Company.

[132] Craig, C. (2019). Pastoral Sex Addiction Professional (PSAP) Training. International Institute for Trauma & Addiction Professionals. February.

We can do this without condoning harmful behavior. Normalize, normalize, normalize. Validate, validate, validate.

Some of us, through our training, our own black and white thinking, or wanting to "get it right," may have grown up with the perspective that the goal is to make as few mistakes as possible in life. This puts a lot of pressure on us to perform and can create a sense of perfectionism. Perfectionism is different than maturity. God anticipates that we will make mistakes. He knows this is a part of being human, and He wants to help us grow, rather than expecting us to be perfect. The Spirit of God is helping us go from immaturity to maturity.[133]

In his book, *Changes that Heal*, Henry Cloud makes a great point about our faith communities being safe places. "It is interesting to compare a legalistic church with a good AA [Alcoholics Anonymous] group. In the church, it is culturally unacceptable to have problems; that is called being sinful. In the AA group, it is culturally unacceptable to be perfect; that is called denial. In one setting people look better but get worse, and in the other, they look worse but get better. Certainly there are good churches and poor AA groups, but because of a lack of grace and truth in some churches, Christians have had to go elsewhere to find healing."[134]

The same could be said of our family environments. Secrecy and perfectionism set us up to hide our mistakes. In our families, whether faith-based or not, sometimes our unwritten rules teach us to hide behind the mask of a perfect family or an "ideal" we may want to portray. Being encouraged to hide rather than being open and humble about mistakes teaches our children to wear masks.

---

[133] John 14:26

[134] Cloud, H. (2003). *Changes That Heal: How to Understand Your Past to Ensure a Healthier Future*. Grand Rapids, MI: Zondervan.

CHAPTER 8: FOCUS ON GROWTH NOT PERFECTION

What we model and what we say create belief systems (true or false beliefs) that we carry with us both consciously and subconsciously.[135]

People wear masks because they don't believe they will be loved if they are truly known. We have a choice whether we want to create an environment of conformity—where we modify our behavior to meet expectations or to "fit in"—or environments of true transformation, being led by our internal values.[136]

If we teach and model that we are expected to make mistakes, that's a completely different starting point. It is easy to have a relationship with our child's behavior, instead of their heart. Remember, the behavior reflects something going on inside of them. When it pushes our button of disrespect or inadequacy, it can seem like it is something different. We need to remind ourselves it is meeting a need they may not even perceive.

What we want to teach are natural consequences for behavior and how to repair relationship when we make mistakes.

RUPTURE, REPAIR, AND RE-DO

It's actually a very important part of a child's development and security to help them learn repair—making a mistake and still being okay—and working together to fix it.

Dr. Tian Dayton, a renowned psychologist and author, has written a book called *Emotional Sobriety*, and shares her perspective this way: "We needn't fear problems or misunderstandings if we learn how to quickly and conscientiously repair them."[137]

---

[135] Dye, M. (2012). *The Genesis Process: For Change Groups, Book 1 and 2, Individual Workbook* (4th ed.). Auburn, CA: Michael Dye.

[136] Grace Network International Training (2014). Creating Environments of Grace.

[137] Dayton, T. (2007). *Emotional Sobriety: From Relationship Trauma to Resilience and Balance.* Deerfield Beach, FL: Health Communications, Inc.

For example, we can handle a common situation like accidentally spilling milk by cleaning it up together, sending the message that mistakes can be repaired and that this is normal. Mistakes can be corrected and can even be a source of learning. It doesn't cause a disconnect in relationship. We can reinforce that mistakes don't cause us to lose relationship or closeness with the parent. We don't have to be afraid of a momentary rupture in relationship.

WHEN THE MESSAGE IS MORE INSTRUCTIVE, INSTEAD OF PUNITIVE, IT HELPS OUR CHILDREN RESOLVE THE SHAME, WHICH CREATES NEW NEURAL WIRING, AS OTHER LEARNING DOES. It teaches that flexibility can become a part of how we relate to other human beings. What an incredible gift when we offer flexibility to ourselves and to others.

The process of rupture and repair is a common and normal experience all throughout life. Experiencing it actually produces growth and helps our child mature.

This then translates into our belief system and the message we believe when there are larger mistakes or disconnects throughout our lives. "We can relax [not be so protective], experiment [see what safety looks like], and be ourselves in relationships if we feel that we can make mistakes."

This is such good advice and easily expands into the area of healthy sexuality and teaching it to our kids. When our kids makes a mistake, such as using inappropriate language or misusing technology, we have the opportunity to help them own the mistake and consequences of it and make it right if others are involved. The important part of this is walking through the repair with them.

My wife and I have always believed in helping our children with mistakes when there is a small problem and the consequences are

CHAPTER 8: FOCUS ON GROWTH NOT PERFECTION

minimal, even being grateful for the opportunity to teach them at that point, rather than waiting until the consequences could have a far greater impact. I would rather intervene with instruction early, instead of the possibility of behaviors continuing into their adulthood. Over the years, I have had so many conversations with men and women in their 30s, 40s, 50s, and even into their 70s, who have struggled with areas of sexuality and addiction. What if they could have gotten help sooner? I'd rather deal with something when it's a problem, than after it becomes a lifelong pattern.

MASTURBATION

Most of us don't have proactive conversations with our kids about masturbation. This is an area in which most of our adolescent boys and many of our adolescent girls will struggle.

Reflect back to whether this was a conversation you had with your own parent(s). What I've found, most likely, is that it wasn't.

Awareness of sexual feelings and our bodies is a natural part of development we don't talk about. Natural doesn't always mean normal. How do we make this a growth area for our child without creating the shame that usually drives this behavior underground? I have put a lot of thought into this because of my own experience as an adolescent and my heart to help my kids grow through this stage.

When I was younger, I worked with the youth at my church. I had a group of 25 high school boys and I gave them this assignment. Go home and talk to your dads about the subject of masturbation. Tell your dad that in the next three weeks, Rodney's going to talk about exposure to pornography and masturbation, and he wanted me to know your opinion about the subject before our next meeting. I'm quite sure the students never had a homework assignment like this before! The next week when they came back, I asked them, "How did your conversations go with your dad?" Out of the 25 of them, only two had the conversation. They were brothers and I think they kind of ganged up on their dad. Or together, they may have had more courage to talk about the subject.

How sad that in a faith community we don't have open dialog about our sexuality. I knew most of these dads, and they were really good men. I'm not saying this to condemn them in any way. I'm simply saying, we don't know how to talk about this subject. We can't discuss these things. Most dads wouldn't know what to answer. They probably would have said, "I agree with whatever Rodney says." Most weren't raised having these conversations. As parents, we are often more comfortable having the youth leader or someone else have the conversation with our kids. This goes back to my point on parents taking the responsibility for educating their children and teaching their own values. It's not a subject we can ignore.

It's important that we are educated and then make decisions based on our personal values. This will help us determine how we want to communicate to our children about masturbation. Remember that shame, secrecy, and isolation are destructive and often very common when we deal with the area of masturbation. Christ doesn't directly address this subject in Scripture, but there are some guiding principles.

As we look at differing views on masturbation, let's start by looking at it from a medical perspective. Here are some thoughts compiled from WebMD.[138]

The medical community did not always see masturbation in the light that it sees it now. Historically, they saw it as either

---

[138] Robinson, J. (2018). *Your Guide to Masturbation*. WebMD Medical Reference. Retrieved from https://www.webmd.com/sex-relationships/qa/is-masturbation-normal.

CHAPTER 8: FOCUS ON GROWTH NOT PERFECTION

perverse or as a mental health problem. The medical community was influenced primarily by strict religious beliefs. They now consider masturbation a natural and harmless expression of sexuality, both for men and women. It is believed to not be harmful to the body when done in moderation.

If you talked to a medical professional about masturbation, they might share some of these thoughts:

Masturbation is described as self-stimulation usually to the point of orgasm. It's a very common behavior that most young men and women have experienced. Some studies show that 95 percent of males and 89 percent of females reported that they had masturbated.[139] It's a natural part of children exploring their bodies, and often a male or female's first sexual experience.

There are different reasons for masturbation. For some it's a safe alternative to avoid STDs or pregnancy. It's a natural part of adolescence and becoming familiar with your body and sexual feelings. Sometimes a man would be asked to masturbate to give a semen sample for infertility testing or for sperm donation.

Here is where the medical community would agree that it is harmful or problematic:[140]

1. When it inhibits sexual activity with your spouse.
2. When it's done in public.
3. If it causes significant distress to the person.
4. If it becomes compulsive and interferes with daily life and activities.

---

[139] Ibid.
[140] Ibid.

The medical community acknowledges that for some, because of cultural or religious beliefs, masturbation may be labeled wrong or sinful. This can lead to guilt and shame over the behavior. The general population of educators and medical professionals are not going to view masturbation as wrong, when not connected to a behavior that is destructive to the individual or others.

I think starting from a health perspective is valuable. We don't have to agree with everything someone else believes on a subject, but I find it helpful to be open minded. I'm glad the medical community has something to say about it.

Knowing this is a difficult subject and often not talked about, I want to offer a continuum of thought on this and allow you to wrestle with the thoughts and listen to your own heart and conscience.

There are a variety of opinions within the Christian faith on this subject. I want to take some time to unpack several viewpoints from different ends of the spectrum regarding masturbation.

CONTINUUM OF THOUGHT ON MASTURBATION

| Masturbation is always wrong, in any situation, married or single. | Masturbation is a natural part of adolescence and isn't harmful or destructive. |

CONSERVATIVE VIEWPOINT

Now, let's look at the conservative view, which at the most extreme says that masturbation is always wrong, harmful, or sinful. Many conservative voices would say that sexual pleasure, when not tied to

CHAPTER 8: FOCUS ON GROWTH NOT PERFECTION

the marriage relationship, is not what God intended. It almost always involves sexual fantasy and is habit forming. It's a violation of God's design for sex to be between two people in a marriage relationship. Masturbation produces guilt, lack of self-control, and is self-centered. Some would take it to an even further extreme and say masturbation is adultery, and sexuality is only to be used for procreation. Anything that gets in the way of sexual intercourse in the marriage act is wrong. Any sexual activity that isn't focused on the goal of reproduction is not what God intended and is sin. In the past, this definition has included birth control, abortion, and masturbation.

A way I have heard this shared is that masturbation is always wrong (sinful) whether you are married or single. Here is the argument: God gave us sex for the sole purpose of bonding, pleasure, and procreation in a covenant relationship—between a husband and wife—called marriage. Therefore, any use of our sexual organs (mind and/or body) outside of its original intent would be wrong or sinful.

LIBERAL VIEWPOINT

A healthy parent or educator within the faith community with a liberal viewpoint would have this point of view on masturbation: if there is a respect of self and others, it is not wrong. The body is inherently good and no parts of it are bad. We touch ourselves and are familiar with other parts of our own bodies, so masturbation is no different. Our bodies get pleasure from all kinds of activities, such as stimulation from all of our senses—the smell of good food, the warmth of the sun, a physical experience of exercise or massage. This group would most likely see fantasy, orgasm, and ejaculation as normal, natural behaviors, especially when not tied to unhealthy or destructive behaviors such as pornography.

MODERATE VIEWPOINT

You can see the arguments for either side of this discussion. Maybe you agree or disagree, but I believe there is value in looking at different points of view on this subject. There are also those who take a moderate view from any point along this continuum. I want to give you some thoughts I have heard that fall somewhere within the lines of this spectrum.

Years ago, Dr. Richard Dobbins, a Christian therapist who was a voice in the area of healthy sexuality, gave his thoughts on masturbation.[141] In my opinion, he was somewhat ahead of his time in speaking to the Church in this area. He was a strong advocate for our sexuality being good. In a conference I attended, Dr. Dobbins shared three reasons he viewed masturbation as a violation of Scripture and leading to sin.

1. Matthew 5: "Lust in our hearts," connecting masturbation to porn or with another person outside of marriage.

2. I Corinthians 6: "All things are lawful, but not all things are beneficial, and be careful not to become mastered by anything." Masturbation can certainly become a destructive coping behavior, used to self-medicate. It can become controlling and "master" a person.

3. I Corinthians 7: when a husband or wife would rather meet their own needs sexually, through masturbation, than to connect with their spouse and meet each other's sexual needs.

---

[141] Dr. Richard Dobbins spoke at a conference I attended.

CHAPTER 8: FOCUS ON GROWTH NOT PERFECTION

I remember Dr. Dobbins speaking on this topic and thinking he brought a lot of clarity to the subject. His advice to a single person was to connect his or her thoughts to the concept of marriage, thank God for their sexuality, and the sexuality they will someday share with a future spouse. He also encouraged, if a spouse is traveling away from their partner and feels the desire to masturbate, they should discuss this first with their partner. If both partners are in agreement, they would choose to connect their sexual thoughts to their spouse. This would reinforce that every time they have a sexual thought they always connect it to their spouse. Dr. Dobbins emphasized the importance of parents talking to their children about masturbation because so many kids are confused and troubled by it.

In one of his books, Dr. Dobbins writes: "Openly discussing masturbation and sexual fantasy with your teens will help them avoid the explosive damage sexual misbehavior can bring."[142] His prime concern is that the youth, during masturbation, will use either pornographic pictures or fantasies involving a specific person. Their brain will train itself to link the sexual stimulation with the specific fantasy. This can cause a need for pornography to be carried over into their married life. However, if they direct a fantasy toward their future spouse, "...then there is nothing morally wrong with it."[143] For the teen, "The spiritual issue is the fantasy accompanying the activity, not the activity itself."[144]

---

[142] Dobbins, R. (2006). Teaching Your Children the Truth About Sex. Lake Mary, FL: Siloam Press. 29-32.

[143] Ibid.

[144] Ibid.

Here is how I would summarize some of Dr. Dobbins thinking:
- Masturbation is a common part of growing up.
- Masturbation is dangerous when used with pornography or objectifying a person.
- If choosing to masturbate, connect your thought to your future spouse.
- Ask God for grace, if needed, to overcome feelings of guilt or shame.
- Neither condone nor condemn masturbation.
- Parents, talk to your kids about your own experiences with masturbation during your teen years.

Here is another perspective, from Dr. James Dobson, founder of Focus on the Family. For years, in his *Preparing for Adolescence Series*, he taught that masturbation could be a part of growing through our adolescent years, when not connected to pornography.

"It is my opinion that masturbation is not much of an issue with God. It is a normal part of adolescence which involves no one else. It does not cause disease. It does not produce babies, and Jesus did not mention it in the Bible. I'm not telling you to masturbate, and I hope you won't feel the need for it. But if you do, it is my opinion that you should not struggle with guilt over it. Why do I tell you this? Because I deal with so many Christian young people who are torn apart with guilt over masturbation; they want to stop and just can't. I would like to help you avoid that agony."[145]

---

[145] Dobson, J. (2005). Preparing for Adolescence: How to Survive the Coming Years of Change. Ventura, CA: Gospel Light.

CHAPTER 8: FOCUS ON GROWTH NOT PERFECTION

Psychologists Cliff and Joyce Penner share their opinion, as well.[146] They state that because masturbation is such a global issue and has been so common throughout history, it can be a normal part of development. They warn that masturbation can become a compulsive habit which can become addictive and destructive. They reinforce that masturbation is always wrong when connected to pornography.

For those of us who have used sex, porn, and masturbation as a coping device to avoid pain and trauma, masturbation can clearly be seen as wrong, destructive, and addictive. SAA (Sex Addicts Anonymous) describes sobriety as abstaining from sex with others or one's self, sex outside of marriage (one man and one woman), and progressing in our battle with lust.[147]

CONCLUSION ON CONTINUUM

All of these viewpoints are simply perspectives or paradigms with which we can agree or disagree.

Wrestle with these thoughts. Look up Scripture or principles that support your view on masturbation or why you disagree with a particular view. Ask questions about it to yourself and others. Discuss with your spouse and/or other mature adults who you trust. Speak with a counselor, educator, mentor, or trusted friend about it.

Remember, even within the Christian faith, there are over thirty thousand different denominations worldwide, because we all see and interpret Scripture differently. Seek to understand the heart of God, which we see clearly through the lens of Christ.

---

[146] Penner, C. & Penner, J. (2003). *The Gift of Sex: A Guide to Sexual Fulfillment.* Nashville, TN: W Publishing Group.

[147] Sex Addicts Anonymous. Sobriety. Retrieved from https://saa-recovery.org/our-program/sobriety/.

OPEN COMMUNICATION ABOUT THIS TOPIC IS CRUCIAL AND THE WAY FORWARD TO HELPING OUR KIDS AND OUR CULTURE TACKLE THIS TOPIC.

You may not agree with all of these perspectives, but you get the opportunity to share with your kids your beliefs and the moral reason behind these beliefs.

SHAME AND SECRECY

I have clearly stated that masturbation can become a destructive and addictive behavior. A place where our faith can be challenged is when we create shame around masturbation and we feel that we have to keep it a secret. Therefore, we believe we have to hide it. This can continue to grow and become a negative pattern for us.

If your child feels guilt about masturbation, help them learn how to deal with the guilt, so it doesn't become shame. Help them manage their sexual feelings and actions in a better way.

HYPERFOCUSING

Beyond whether masturbation is right or wrong, some kids can simply become hyperfocused on it because they don't have other things that make them feel a sense of worth and value. How does this happen? If a young person is struggling at school, didn't make the team, is being bullied, family relationships aren't going well, feels isolated or struggles making friends, they could become hyperfocused on masturbation—using it to cope with unwanted thoughts, feelings, and emotions.

In an oversexualized culture, our kids may begin to masturbate to the point where it becomes the one area in their life creating positive feelings. Without their awareness, masturbation can

CHAPTER 8: FOCUS ON GROWTH NOT PERFECTION

become an addictive pattern, providing a hit of dopamine to the brain with every experience.[148]

Help your children find wins in many different aspects of their lives, such as sports, music, art, schoolwork, youth group, or an extracurricular activity or club. Whatever their bent is, help them find it. More than anything, reinforce relationships with family and others.

WE HAVE TO HELP OUR KIDS DEVELOP HOLISTICALLY AND FIND HEALTHIER WAYS TO COPE WITH STRESS AND DISAPPOINTMENT IN LIFE.

Hyperfocusing can also be connected to trauma, which may or may not include sexual abuse. In these cases, masturbation can be used as either self-soothing or reenactment of the abuse. In cases of trauma, it is so important to connect your child with a trauma professional, so they are able to heal and reduce the potential for long-term effects.

DON'T BE SILENT

Whatever you do, don't be silent when it comes to talking to your kids about masturbation. Have an opinion and share it. Be willing to explain your values and the reason why you have come to believe the way you do. Children want to know the moral reasons behind things, not just because "I said so." This will help them when they are making their own moral decisions.

Every person has their own experiences surrounding masturbation. If a child experiences abuse, early exposure to pornography, or shame-based messages they will react to their

---

[148] Doidge, N. (2007). *The Brain That Changes Itself: Stories of Personal Triumph from the Frontiers of Brain Science.* New York, NY: Penguin Books.

trauma in a specific way. For a minority, they will not masturbate in adolescence. For some, masturbation will be an experience but not a pattern. It will naturally fade in interest.

Even in the same family, masturbation could be a different experience. My wife and I each have a different experience with masturbation in adolescence.

As a parent, you get to share your own experience with your child. Here are some guiding principles around masturbation:

- Maintain open conversation with your child about their sexuality.
- Mistakes are how we learn and grow. Keep a growth mindset.[149]
- All of us are going from immaturity to maturity in our decision-making.
- Let your "moral reason" be more than "because I said so."
- Honest relationship is always better than shameful isolation.
- Elevate the value of every human as a person, not an object to be used.
- Clearly share with your kids the dangers of pornography connected to masturbation.
- If your kids are older, share your own experience about masturbation.
- If a child is compulsively masturbating, seek professional outside help.

---

[149] Dweck, C. (2006). *Mindset: The New Psychology of Success.* New York, NY: Ballantine Books.

CHAPTER 8: FOCUS ON GROWTH NOT PERFECTION

IMMATURITY AND MATURITY

Helping our children understand our viewpoints and perspective on masturbation—allowing the Spirit to guide them in making decisions about how to handle this area of their life and helping them progress—is about going from immaturity to maturity. **SO MUCH OF LIFE IS ABOUT THE PROCESS OF MATURITY AND GROWTH, NOT THE PURSUIT OF PERFECTION.** Helping our kids see that life is about growing and moving toward maturity is a great concept—that our mistakes are opportunities for us to move toward this goal. Whether in masturbation or managing our sexuality, or discovering our purpose and life's calling, this is the goal: moving from immaturity to maturity.

I'm so glad we are not alone. God is also working in us toward this same goal.

CHAPTER 8

TRY THIS!

THIS WEEK, SHARE A STORY WITH ONE OF YOUR CHILDREN ABOUT AN AREA OF YOUR LIFE WHERE YOU HAVE GROWN OR ARE CURRENTLY GROWING.

QUESTIONS

1 | Take a look inward at how you handle your own mistakes. Are you okay with growth not perfection in your life? In what way was perfectionism part of your upbringing?

2 | How safe do you believe you are as a parent to your child(ren)? How safe is your home environment? Would your family agree? What is one thing you could do to change or keep improving your level of safety?

3 | What is a specific area you would like to give yourself or someone in your family grace to continue to grow?

4 | After reading the pages on the Continuum of Thought on Masturbation, explain your thoughts.

5 | How would you like to share this concept with your children?

CHAPTER 9

KEEP MODELING

Somewhere along the journey of parenting, I seemed to go from my little ones' hero to a season where I wondered if anyone was actually listening to what I said. Shouldn't the years of navigating my own adolescence and focus on growth as an adult have prepared me to have some "fatherly wisdom" to dole out? There were times in my kids' teenage years where they weren't that excited to hear these words of wisdom. My wife would continually remind me, "What you model is more important than what you say."

Humility, honesty, being a lifelong learner, not living in shame, owning our mistakes, fostering deep connections, asking for help, managing our sexuality in healthy ways...modeling these behaviors are the best gifts we can offer to our kids. *We must be smoking what we're selling*, so to speak.

NONVERBAL COMMUNICATION

Remember, communication isn't always verbal. **Our children watch everything we do.** They watch us and they mimic our behaviors. This is how a baby first learns to speak. They are watching us and others form words. When I was young I thought people were born with certain accents. I didn't realize this was a learned behavior. When kids are young they will often say phrases that mimic exactly what we, as parents, say and take on our mannerisms. Kids are very perceptive. They are watching if our words and actions are consistent. They are aware when our words and values contradict our behavior, and this can be very confusing for them. An obvious example is if we, as parents, use profane language and then reprimand our children for doing the same.

Our values are the things most important to us; what we "give value to," our principles, or standards of behavior.

Inconsistency in our behavior does not go unnoticed. This is where the framework and the construct of our kid's little world starts and where they begin to develop beliefs and values. Out of these beliefs and values come their choices and behaviors. Their choices and behaviors may be motivated through many things. Sometimes fear—fear of punishment or disappointing their parents—or they may be motivated by a value they have developed as their own.

OUR CHILDREN ARE LEARNING HOW THE WORLD WORKS BY THE ACTIONS OF THOSE AROUND THEM, AND ESPECIALLY THEIR MOST SIGNIFICANT RELATIONSHIPS: PARENTS, FAMILY MEMBERS, TEACHERS, NEIGHBORS, PEERS, AND FAITH COMMUNITIES. They are not just learning in the area of sexuality, but in areas of relationship, forgiveness, personal vulnerability, and so many other areas—they are all connected. When our children are small they may not even understand our words, but they are always observing and imitating our actions. When they are teenagers they may tune us out or act like they don't hear us, but they are still "picking up what we're laying down."

Every parent is somewhat aware of the way that their children imitate them. From infancy children learn. They build their own story onto what they learn from parents and important people in their world.

CHAPTER 9: KEEP MODELING

As children, we pick up on our parents' values long before we can even understand them for ourselves. As we grow older, we sometimes question these values. As we enter our teenage years, the values of our peers have a strong influence on most of us. As young adults preparing to leave our parents' home, we again test our own values.

Some parents teach their children to question things and develop their own sense of values. Other parents tend to want their children to take on their own values and don't give them much room to develop values for themselves. I have seen this issue play out when children leave home for the first time, sometimes for college. If they have not developed their own values, it can feel overwhelming for them to make decisions when they are not under their parents' rules. My wife and I would rather have our kids struggle while they are in our home and we can be there to process and navigate with them.

This is why it is so important to have conversations with our kids about all areas and aspects of life—to ask them what they think and let them question why we (as parents) believe the way we do or live our lives the way we do.

This is one of the reasons the phrase "actions speak louder than words" exists. As a parent, this can feel scary because we do so many things automatically. **WE HAVE TO LEARN TO BE INTENTIONAL IN WHAT WE DO AND HOW WE RESPOND TO SITUATIONS.** This seems like something we are all aware of, and yet sometimes, in our busy and overwhelmed lives, we don't stop to think about the impact we're having and to be intentional about what we are modeling.

Studies and more recent developments of brain science have confirmed and explained things we already observe.[150] The concept of behavioral modeling was introduced in the 1960s, through an experiment: in front of their child, an adult modeled either gentle or aggressive play with toys and then left the room. While left on their own, many children repeated their parent's behavior.

Our children watch our behaviors. They model what they observe. In so many ways, whether we recognize it or not, we are creating mini-mes: little clones of ourselves.

This is the power of generational patterns and what we, as parents, are behaviorally passing on to our kids.

GROWTH AS A PARENT

Sometimes, we haven't been growing very well as a parent. We may not be continuing to mature as an adult. The truth is, none of us are going to do this perfectly. Parents are imperfect. Fortunately, kids are resilient. We will make mistakes. We will let our kids and ourselves down. The goal isn't to get it right 100 percent of the time. We want the big picture of our lives to model our values and to be authentic. We want to learn what to do when we make mistakes—how to repair.

My son and I had tension during his middle school and high school years. For a long period of time, there was no real conversation, a big disconnect, and some real struggles. This was not just for days or weeks, but went on for months and years.

There were tears, raised voices, and disrespectful behavior that affected not only our relationship, but our whole family's dynamic. With a lack of connection, hearts grow cold toward

---

[150] Nolen, J. (2015). *Bobo doll experiment*. Encyclopedia Britannica, Inc. Retrieved from https://www.britannica.com/event/Bobo-doll-experiment.

CHAPTER 9: KEEP MODELING

each other. This is what happened to us. I allowed my heart to disconnect because the rejection I felt in the relationship hurt so much. This was my first son. The little guy I had played *Lion King* with, who meant the world to me, that I became apathetic toward. The pain was so deep and the sense of failure was so strong that I began to shut down in my feelings. I hate to say it, but this was survival for me.

I knew my son was going through a difficult season, but our disconnect kept me on the outside and kept him in isolation. Instead of helping, I was making it worse. My wife and I went to counseling to get help. I was reaching out for as much help as I could get. At first, the counseling we received was more punitive. If you've ever had a difficult interaction with one of your kids, you know that trying different things, being more strict, less strict, just doing the best you know how to do doesn't always feel effective. Sometimes it seems like nothing works. So much second-guessing. You are trying to motivate them through different approaches, sometimes back and forth between discipline, positive affirmation or punishment, and negative consequences for their actions. What worked for one child doesn't seem to work for another, and there doesn't seem to be a parent manual for perfect parenting through the seasons of your child's life.

At one point, my wife and I had gotten more strict with rules and boundaries, and my son said, "You're the worst parent in the world. I can't believe the church lets you help parents." I stood on the stairs below him and said, "Right now, no one knows that I need help being a parent more than I do." Sometimes I wondered if the "fence could ever be mended" or if it was irreparable. It felt like we were permanently stuck and it might always be this way.

Over several years and a long process, I stopped trying to change my son. I focused on my growth and began the slow process of building back the trust we had lost. I practiced personal vulnerability and owning my part of the relationship that was handled wrong. I had to ask what part of our struggle was mine to own and lead the way toward repair and restoration.

I've learned that once a heart becomes hardened, for whatever reason, if met with the right conditions, over time, it can be mended—the feelings of love and connection can return.

WE CAN NEVER CONTROL THE RESPONSE OF THE OTHER PERSON, BUT WE DO HAVE CONTROL OVER OUR RESPONSE. THIS IS THE WORK OF RECOVERY IN ALL ASPECTS OF LIFE.

Many years later, through tears, honesty, and many conversations—listening and grieving our hurts together—we were able to take a few steps forward. We took responsibility for the pain we caused each other.

This past week, my son called me after a job interview in Phoenix, Arizona. He shared with me the details of the interview. They asked him who had impacted him the most in his life and why. He told them about his dad's vulnerability and said, "My dad always taught me that "Healthy people seek help, and seeking help is a sign of our wisdom, not of weakness.'"

Today, this kid is one of my best friends.

HONESTY ABOUT OUR STRUGGLE

We can tell our kids, "Be honest about your struggles," but if we're not honest about *our* struggles, we're not sending a healthy message. This can be easier said than done. Sometimes parents even think it's better to look strong in front of their kids.

CHAPTER 9: KEEP MODELING

Several years ago, my wife and I chose to share our story of navigating through my addiction and the betrayal my wife experienced with our kids, as well as the many years of our healing journey. They were preschool age and younger when we went through disclosure and started the journey of healing together, and, at the time, we only shared enough to let them know that mommy and daddy were going through something sad and asking people to help us.

My wife and I chose to share a more in-depth version when they were ages 14-19, and, as I said earlier, looking back we wish we would have shared it a little sooner. Over time, it's been such a gift to see what this level of transparency has produced in our family.

We didn't know what to expect in their reactions, and every child is different in how they process, but it brought a definite shift in connection in our family. Our daughter, who was 19 at the time, said, "Dad, I'm glad you saw yourself valuable enough to get help."

MODELING HUMILITY

We can understand humility better if we first define pride and false humility. Here is my favorite way of looking at the concept of humility: we can have pride, false humility, or humility. Pride says, "Hi, I'm Rodney. Here are my strengths, and I have no weaknesses." False humility says, "Hi, I'm Rodney. Here are my weaknesses, and I have no strengths." Humility says, "Hi, I'm Rodney. Here are my strengths and here are my weaknesses."

My kids would not say they had perfect parents. In fact, in our family, we are all honest about being broken people in different areas. My kids would quickly tell you that we have let them down, made mistakes, and even openly shared mistakes we've made in our lives—mistakes they weren't necessarily aware of.

But what my kids would say is that their parents are committed to growth—that we don't "pretend" to have all of the answers. We keep growing.

I have heard many stories where a dad and his son are estranged and neither will speak to each other. In my opinion, much of this is the parent's pride getting in the way. Being a leader means going first. In my opinion, parents need to be the one letting go of pride and leading the way.

As parents, we have to be willing to lead in humility. It's not about being right. It is about the deeper value of connection. Yes, the risk of rejection is sometimes high and usually very painful, but humility is the way forward. Humility never looks bad on us. My family has never said, "We hate when Dad's humble. We love when he's prideful and arrogant." My arrogance has been repulsive, but humility looks good on everyone.

A few years back, I received a Father's Day card from my teenage son. He signed it, "Mom and I are proud of the man you are becoming." In his adolescent years, as he was growing into a young man, his mom had signed his card this way many times. I think my wife was trying to use positive reinforcement.

It's a wonderful thing when you see your 17-year-old son start to mature, but it's even better when a 40-year-old father continues to mature.

MODELING TOWARD EACH OTHER

The goal of parenting isn't just being focused on our kids, but good parenting is when we model loving our partner in healthy and respectful ways. Some people say, "Well, we had a bad marriage, but we were great parents." I say, not true—being a great parent is learning to love your spouse well and modeling it

CHAPTER 9: KEEP MODELING

for your children. If you are divorced or a single parent, it is still about being loving and respectful toward your children's other parent, toward those around you, toward family members, and leaders. Loving doesn't mean you agree with someone or don't have healthy boundaries. It's all connected. We, as humans, are connected to each other.

WE HAVE THE OPPORTUNITY TO MODEL FOR OUR KIDS A LOVING AFFECTIONATE RELATIONSHIP WITH EACH OTHER BASED ON HOW WE SPEAK AND INTERACT WITH EACH OTHER. All of these things make deep impressions on our kids from early childhood, through teenage years, and on into adulthood.

When my children were young, my wife and I shared with our kids that, "Mom and Dad have a special kind of love." We modeled touch, affection, and positive emotions toward each other.

My wife and I wanted our kids to feel the safety and strength of their parents' marriage. Sometimes there is a tendency to be child-focused. After all, our kids take a lot of our attention in their younger years and even through adolescence, and we sometimes don't have a lot of time to invest in our marriage. If a marriage is struggling, the parents may focus primarily on their child. Sometimes, after the kids leave the home, the parents look at each other and think, *I don't know you* or *I don't know if I even like you*. In this situation, we sometimes see a marriage end, which is surprising— they have been married 20-30 years, but they have grown apart. They have become independent instead of interdependent.

Some parents worry about being separated from their children. They don't take an evening, weekend, or a trip away from their kids. They may have to call and check on their children constantly when they aren't with them. Not being entirely child-focused is helpful to your kids. It actually promotes security for them. Having other healthy relationships besides our children, with our spouse and others, is very important.

Our children will not be harmed by taking a reasonable amount of time to focus on the marriage. In fact, our children will feel a sense of security and safety in seeing a strong connection between their parents.

This applies if you are single as well—to take time for self-care and relationship with others is an incredibly healthy way of modeling to your children.

Establishing focused time with each other, whether it's five minutes of sitting and talking on the couch after work (setting boundaries for a few minutes where the children can practice not interrupting) or getting away for a vacation together, is a great practice.

Early on, my wife and I established a budget for taking a trip every five years, just Mom and Dad, no kids, as far away and as long as we could, with grandpa and grandma in charge.

You may not be able to do this or may be able to do this more often than we could, but that was one of our attempts to invest in our relationship outside of the parent role. You may have to be creative.

My wife and I used to swap childcare with friends on a Friday night every now and then. We both had three kids, and we would bring our kids over, dressed in pajamas, for movie night and to fall asleep there. This allowed us to go out a night without the cost of babysitting. Instead of seeing our limits, it was an intentional way to have time together. Sometimes we would just help our three kids get set up with a cartoon in the family room and sneak off for a few minutes. With three kids, five and under, it really was sometimes, "five minutes of intimacy." Five minutes alone with your spouse may be a valued commodity.

CHAPTER 9: KEEP MODELING

One of the funniest stories with our kids happened when our daughter was 6, our son Austin was 4, and his brother was almost a year old. The kids were watching a movie in the bonus room, and Traci and I snuck off for what we would refer to as "a quick nap" in our bedroom. A couple minutes later, there was a knock at the door, and we asked, "What do you want?" We heard Austin's little voice, "I've got something for you." We said, "Just a minute, Austin. Leave it there for us." He paused for a moment and then we heard him say, "I can't. It'll crawl away." We looked at each other and burst out laughing. Austin had carried his brother downstairs and wanted to leave him with us. I guess he wasn't too pleased that we stuck him and his sister with their baby brother. Suddenly, the intimate moment became hilarious.

There is a joy and an awkwardness in trying to parent and still maintain an intimate relationship with your spouse. My wife and I kept working on practical ways of modeling in our marriage and keeping our connection strong as a team: going on dates, taking trips together, supporting each other, and sometimes even kissing or flirting with each other in front of the kids. When the kids were really young, they would giggle and be embarrassed, and when they were older they would tease and basically say, "You two need to get a room." In high school and young adulthood our sons would tease us about our flirting or "why we locked the bedroom door," and even though it seemed weird, it was actually really healthy for them. It's good for kids to witness the nonsexual flirting and attraction their parents have toward each other. It can set up the context for a loving, affectionate future marriage for them.

We didn't share details around our sexual intimacy, but I would often joke with them when they were older and say, "You guys are really going to like marriage someday." This created an openness without being inappropriate.

This might not be your style or personality. You may have a different approach and be more private by nature, but modeling the importance of your marriage and letting your kids into this world is valuable, in whatever way you choose to do so.

When we are building up our spouse in a multitude of ways it shows respect. We are showing our kids how to have a romantic relationship beyond the act of sex. We want our children surrounded by people who are modeling how to have nonsexual intimacy, as well as discussing what it means to be sexually intimate. Our kids are impacted by how we interact and connect with our spouse and other relationships in our lives.

My wife and I did our best to keep modeling and growing in our day-to-day relationship with each other in front of our kids. This doesn't mean we never argued, disagreed, or irritated each other in front of them. Our kids witnessed all of this as well. We also modeled how to resolve conflict. We modeled well and sometimes we modeled poorly. Sometimes our kids held us accountable for how we talked to each other or patterns that weren't healthy, and they still do to this day. They will say "Dad, you are kind of overreacting today" or "Mom, I think Dad just needs you to listen to him. You're talking over him." We even have a sign in our family we started jokingly using when one of us isn't "aware" of how we are acting. We developed it when one of us was rambling on without knowing it, and it has stuck with us. It's a gentle gesture to say, "You might want to stop and be mindful of how you are coming across right now." We have done it in a way that we can laugh at ourselves, because really all of us have poor ways of communicating sometimes. We don't have to shame anyone or ourselves.

The best thing that we, as parents, can give our kids is for them to see that when we make mistakes it is not the end of it.

CHAPTER 9: KEEP MODELING

We are committed to growing. This is one of the main reasons I started this book with the chapter Pursue Personal Health. This is really the best thing we model and can't build on the rest of life's tools very well without personal health.

One of my kids, when they were in junior high, told me they were talking with another friend about their parents' marriages. My child told their friend, "My parents work on their marriage." Somehow the message was getting across to our kids that growing in marriage was normal, took hard work and effort, and there was value in being intentional about it.

In the area of sexuality, when kids see their parents married for 10, 20, or 30 years and still lovingly connected, it sets them up for connecting their sexuality to their future partner. If children rarely or never see their parents having a sexual attraction toward each other—through healthy physical affection—they will likely think their sexuality is made for their girlfriend, boyfriend, pornography, or the false messages they see in the media. Healthy sexuality isn't the loudest message in our culture. They may struggle to connect the concept of their sexuality with marriage.

If I could give you one piece of advice: keep working on your own personal growth and growth in your marriage. **WHETHER SINGLE OR MARRIED, IN A HEALTHY OR UNHEALTHY MARRIAGE, WHAT YOU CAN CONTROL IS YOUR OWN PERSONAL GROWTH.**

If you are raising your child in a single parent home, it's so important to have healthy community around you. Whether it's grandparents, aunts, uncles, church mentors, or friends, make sure your children are around healthy marriages, where they can witness what a healthy marriage should look like. Depending on your child's age, it is very valuable to have open communication about the challenges you faced in your marriage, or as a single parent. This goes back to what I mentioned about honesty and humility. It's okay if you don't have the "perfect scenario." Really, none of us do. All of the choices and traumas we go through in life get in the way of our "ideal scenario." Your children will learn through watching you handle difficulties as much or more than how you handle successes. Give them a loving, affectionate home and build strong relationships around you as a family.

MODELING WITH OTHERS

From the beginning of our marriage, my wife and I have looked to individuals and couples who are farther down the road than us, whose marriage, family, and raising of kids we admired. We spent time with them, observed what they did, and talked about it together.

Over the years, this is where many of my thoughts—many that you're reading in this book—have come from: the observing of others. My wife and I were intentional about learning from what others did "right" and from the mistakes they made, including our own parents, adding it to what we taught our children.

My wife and I were not the only models in our children's lives. It's not realistic to think that everything we modeled will definitely be embraced, but we do impact our children significantly throughout their lives.

There are weak links in the way we do things as individuals and as families. These are the things that we, as parents, pass down in life. Our kids need to pick up strengths from others and learn from the mistakes of others, as well as from us. This is why being around a community of healthy people is so important.

In addition, because of our belief in "paying it forward," my wife and I also try to have couples and families who are not

CHAPTER 9: KEEP MODELING

as far through life as we are, to pass on some of the lessons we have learned—both our successes and our failures. We do this by investing in younger couples, leading groups, and simply encouraging parents who are in the middle of the child-raising years. Remember, we don't have time to make all of the mistakes ourselves. Learn from others and pass along the wisdom.

Pouring into others is a huge part of our own recovery. It's an impactful part of modeling to others, their children, as well as our children. This is one of the reasons to keep parents involved in their kid's schools, extracurricular activities, and church groups. The modeling we do for those coming behind us allows us to be the "tribal elders."

I mentioned earlier and gave some examples of parents who have taken the approach to modeling seriously, and didn't leave it up to teachers and other leaders.

PASSING ON THE GOOD AND THE BAD - GENERATIONALLY SPEAKING

The concept of generational patterns comes from Old Testament Scripture and it's easy for us to observe how traits are passed down from generation to generation. At a training my wife and I attended, the instructor was talking about this: how Jewish families historically lived in the same home with several generations and would have picked up on these patterns directly from their ancestors.[151]

We know this to be true, often from the modeling in our own families. Children mimic what their parents model, which could be alcoholism, abuse, lying, pursuing money, procrastination,

---

[151] Riemersma, J. (2019). Pastoral Sex Addiction Professional (PSAP) Training. International Institute for Trauma & Addiction Professionals. February.

anxiety, perfectionism, and more. Children also mimic positive behaviors: generosity, kindness, honesty, strong work ethics, gratitude, and hospitality. **WE WILL LIVE OUT PARTS OF WHAT IS MODELED TO US.** This is not literal—we don't pick up every addiction or every favorable trait in our parents and grandparents. But the principle holds true—what we observe in our parent's behaviors often becomes part of our behaviors.

An interesting study of epigenetics explains another way that family traits get passed down.[152] Our life experiences and choices change us and our brain at the DNA level—which also can change the way our DNA expresses itself in future generations. It shows how many of our repetitive patterns get passed down, not only through modeling, but through our genes.

We also pass on false belief systems.[153] Beliefs about ourselves, God, and others that we pick up from our parents and they picked up from their parents. This can be direct statements that they said to us or the stories we wrote in our minds about what we observed and experienced. The entire chain of behaviors, if you will, can be passed down to future generations. If our unhealthy behaviors are not recognized and addressed, processed through counseling or a group experience, this cycle of behaviors—generational patterns—will repeat.

The good news is that God designed us for change and this is true even in the study of epigenetics. When it comes

---

[152] Wiles, J. (Producer), Wiles, T. (Producer), Melin, J. (Producer) & Wiles, J. (Director). (2013). *Conquer Series: The Battle Plan for Purity* [DVD]. United States: KingdomWorks Studios.

[153] Dye, M. (2012). *The Genesis Process: For Change Groups, Book 1 and 2, Individual Workbook* (4th ed.). Auburn, CA: Michael Dye.

CHAPTER 9: KEEP MODELING

to our brain, it is capable of great change.[154] This means we don't have to hold on to the old destructive behaviors from our families. We can learn new behaviors, habits, and traits through our choices and experiences. Then, we have the opportunity to pass on health to our kids. New opposite experiences are a powerful way we change our brain.[155]

Sometimes people explain the trait of blue eyes by saying, "It runs in our family." My wife and I say, "Sarcasm runs in our family," but we have more control over sarcasm than eye color. Sarcasm is clearly something I have passed down to my kids, but I am working on it. I'm also working on passing down to my kids openness and honesty about sexuality. This one is going well.

None of us have it all figured out, but we need to be on the same page in breaking patterns of secrecy. How do we do this? It takes work, intentionality, and supportive counsel and groups to reinforce and encourage the pursuit of healthy living.

We usually have some deep soul work to do over time before we can break free from generational patterns. These are behaviors that have been handed down from generation to generation—affecting how we think, feel, and live—and are sometimes deeply embedded. In fact, we may not even be aware of some of these traits. Taking a look at what was modeled for us, with a spiritual leader or counselor, can help us unravel what has a grip on our family. This helps us break generational patterns so we're not passing unhealthy behaviors on to our children.

---

[154] Wiles, J. (Producer), Wiles, T. (Producer), Melin, J. (Producer) & Wiles, J. (Director). (2013). *Conquer Series: The Battle Plan for Purity* [DVD]. United States: KingdomWorks Studios.

[155] Roberts, T. (2014). *Seven Pillars of Freedom Workbook*. Gresham, OR: Pure Desire Ministries International.

It is helpful to take an inventory, and there are tools and professionals that can help with this process.[156]

> SINCE GOD HAS SO GENEROUSLY LET US IN ON WHAT HE IS DOING, WE'RE NOT ABOUT TO THROW UP OUR HANDS AND WALK OFF THE JOB JUST BECAUSE WE RUN INTO OCCASIONAL HARD TIMES. WE REFUSE TO WEAR MASKS AND PLAY GAMES. WE DON'T MANEUVER AND MANIPULATE BEHIND THE SCENES. AND WE DON'T TWIST GOD'S WORD TO SUIT OURSELVES. RATHER, WE KEEP EVERYTHING WE DO AND SAY OUT IN THE OPEN, THE WHOLE TRUTH ON DISPLAY, SO THAT THOSE WHO WANT TO CAN SEE AND JUDGE FOR THEMSELVES IN THE PRESENCE OF GOD.[157]

As parents, we want to pass on positive traits—things we value. What a beautiful thing that we can change unhealthy behaviors and pass on something new because our brain is plastic and can rewire. We have the opportunity to stop the cycles we don't want to pass on and replace them with new, healthy behaviors.

GIVING BACK AND MAKING AMENDS

If you keep your life, you'll lose it. But if you give it away, you'll find it.[158]

Giving back is a part of the 12-Step approach.[159] Neither my wife or I grew up around the 12-Step process. We have come to

---

[156] Dye, M. (2012). *The Genesis Process: For Change Groups, Book 1 and 2, Individual Workbook* (4th ed.). Auburn, CA: Michael Dye.

[157] 2 Corinthians 4:1-2 MSG

[158] Luke 17:33

[159] Smith, B. & Wilson, B. (1939). *The Big Book of Alcoholics Anonymous.* Asheville, NC: Lark Publishing LLC.

CHAPTER 9: KEEP MODELING

learn that this doesn't mean our families and faith communities didn't have any addictions. It's just that the more "socially accepted" addictions, like overworking, overeating, judgment, and gossip didn't have groups for them. "We're all addicted to our own way of thinking," but we have seen firsthand, and in others close to us, how deeply spiritual the 12-Step process can be. We have found the message and process of the 12-Step approach to be a healthy part of the journey for all of us.

A powerful and transformative step in the 12-Step process—and equally difficult—is the process of making amends to those we've hurt. When our children are young, it's good to start the habit of apologizing to them when needed. This sends a big message to our child and teaches them to apologize to others, and even with their children in the future. **MAKING AMENDS WITH OUR KIDS—ADMITTING WHERE WE MAY HAVE MISSED IT—IS AN INCREDIBLE BEHAVIOR TO MODEL.**

This was something my wife and I saw modeled at various times by our parents, and we sought to do the same. Many times, we have gone back to our children and talked about what went wrong and even, at times, what steps we were making to change when we recognized unhealthy patterns in our behaviors.

It's not just about asking forgiveness but learning to be self-aware and taking steps to make changes in how we respond to others. This is done over a process of time.

Sometimes making amends is about owning our negative sexual history, either prior to marriage or during the marriage. As we get healthy, part of the healing process can be to go back and make it right with others that we have hurt. At times, this is not possible or healthy, but we still have the opportunity to own those mistakes and find healing and forgiveness of ourselves. This can also be a part of the disclosure process with couples and families.[160] I have experienced the positive impact this can have in a family and have seen it lived out in a number of marriages and families I've worked with.

My wife and I say this all the time to our kids: "You saw our marriage and family. It wasn't perfect. Whatever you saw that is healthy, take it with you. Whatever you saw that's unhealthy, leave it here with us; don't take it with you. Find a better way. Learn from our mistakes because you're not going to have time to make them all yourselves."

What if today was your last day on earth? What if this week you were going to receive news that would change everything. Perspective is very valuable. Every day is a gift and we aren't guaranteed tomorrow, so we must learn to live in the present. You are leaving a legacy. Like it or not, you are modeling something! What do you want to leave behind for others to follow?

CELEBRATING SUCCESS

Although we wish we were above making mistakes, my wife and I have learned to grieve the mistakes we made and the ways we wish we would have done things differently. We also take time to celebrate our successes.

We have learned not to take credit for every success and every mistake our children make. They are not entirely succeeding or failing because of everything we did or didn't do. We surely contributed to who they are today. They are imperfect reflections of us, just as we are imperfect reflections of a perfect Creator.

Since it is sometimes easier to look at what we didn't do well, my wife and I often choose to talk about and focus on our

---

[160] Roberts, T. (2014). *Seven Pillars of Freedom Workbook*. Gresham, OR: Pure Desire Ministries International.

CHAPTER 9: KEEP MODELING

kid's successes. Our three children and newly added son-in-law are incredible people. They have a lot of depth—they are open individuals who want to grow and be the best humans they can be. We will always be their biggest cheerleaders, jump up and down at their successes, and say, "Yes, we were co-creators with God in that human being's life!" We have participated in this life with them, just like God invites us to participate with Him.

A favorite author of mine, Richard Rohr, shares an impactful story:

> OUR NEGATIVE AND CRITICAL THOUGHTS ARE LIKE VELCRO, THEY STICK AND HOLD; WHEREAS OUR POSITIVE AND JOYFUL THOUGHTS ARE LIKE TEFLON, THEY SLIDE AWAY. WE HAVE TO DELIBERATELY CHOOSE TO HOLD ON TO POSITIVE THOUGHTS BEFORE THEY 'IMPRINT.' NEUROSCIENCE CAN NOW DEMONSTRATE THE BRAIN INDEED HAS A NEGATIVE BIAS; THE BRAIN PREFERS TO CONSTELLATE AROUND FEARFUL, NEGATIVE, OR PROBLEMATIC SITUATIONS. IN FACT, WHEN A LOVING, POSITIVE, OR UNPROBLEMATIC THING COMES YOUR WAY, YOU HAVE TO SAVOR IT CONSCIOUSLY FOR AT LEAST FIFTEEN SECONDS BEFORE IT CAN HARBOR AND STORE ITSELF IN YOUR 'IMPLICIT MEMORY;' OTHERWISE IT DOESN'T STICK. WE MUST INDEED SAVOR THE GOOD IN ORDER TO SIGNIFICANTLY CHANGE OUR REGULAR ATTITUDES AND MOODS. AND WE NEED TO STRICTLY MONITOR ALL THE 'VELCRO' NEGATIVE THOUGHTS.[161]

---

[161] Rohr, R. (2014). *Embracing An Alternative Orthodoxy.* Denver, CO: Morehouse Education Resources.

As I'm going through the day, I will often stop and remind myself to take 15 seconds to focus on gratitude. I may be alone or on a walk with my wife and say, "See that sunset. I'm going to stop for 15 seconds and let this soak in—store it in my memory." This is how gratitude works. **GRATITUDE IS A PART OF CELEBRATING: CELEBRATING WHAT IS GOOD AND WHAT IS RIGHT IN THE WORLD AND THE PEOPLE AROUND US, INCLUDING OURSELVES.**

It reminds me of a song, "Of all that I've done wrong, I must have done something right."[162] There is so much good in each of our children, and in ourselves, even in the times we can't see it.

---

[162] Carlisle, B. & Thomas, R. (1997). Butterfly Kisses [Recorded by B. Carlisle]. On *Butterfly Kisses (Shades of Grace)* [CD]. United States: MCA Records.

CHAPTER 9
TRY THIS!

THIS WEEK, CHOOSE AN AREA YOU WOULD LIKE TO MODEL DIFFERENTLY. IT COULD BE COMMUNICATION, SELF CARE, VULNERABILITY, OR SHOWING HEALTHY AFFECTION TO YOUR SPOUSE. LET SOMEONE KNOW YOUR COMMITMENT TO THIS CHANGE.

OR

WRITE OUT A PARAGRAPH OR PAGE ON THE LEGACY YOU WOULD LIKE TO LEAVE BEHIND.

QUESTIONS

1 | How important have you made the process of modeling?

2 | What is something your parents modeled for you, positive or negative?

3 | Think of a success you've had in your parenting. Where has modeling along the way produced a positive result?

4 | What is one personal takeaway from this chapter you would like to work on as it pertains to how you want to model?

CHAPTER 10

NEVER TURN AWAY

What's most true about our kids and every human being is that we have intrinsic (built-in) worth and value. We are all made in the image of our Creator, which Scripture states, "is very good."[163] Or as the nanny says to Mae Mobley in the popular movie, *The Help*: "You is kind. You is smart. You is important."[164]

I used to think God turned away from me when I made a mistake—that God's love was conditional. A "holy" God couldn't look on "sinful" humanity. "He loves me, he loves me not," based on my performance. I especially believed this because of the mistakes I had made in the area of sexuality. I believed there would be times God would leave me—that I would be separated from God or He would abandon me. I no longer believe this. I attempt to see God through the lens of Jesus, and I want my kids to be able to do the same. God is exactly like Jesus![165]

---

[163] Genesis 1:27 & 31

[164] Barnathan, M. (Producer), Columbus, C. (Producer), Green, B. (Producer) & Taylor, T. (Director). (2011). *The Help* [Motion Picture]. United States: Walt Disney Studios.

[165] Jersak, B. (2015). *A More Christlike God: A More Beautiful Gospel*. Pasadena, CA: Plain Truth Ministries.

BELIEFS

HOW WE PARENT IS GOING TO REFLECT OUR BELIEF SYSTEM ABOUT OURSELVES, GOD, AND OTHERS. If we don't have a good starting point for this, it will affect everything we do personally and the way we parent. This actually creates the foundation for everything we do as a parent. If we don't feel secure in our relationships, we will model or teach our children to feel insecure, not only in Father God but in their earthly parents. These beliefs will drive our behaviors and influence our children's behaviors.

When our message is shame-based, we will act out of our shame. We often give up on ourselves. We turn away from "us."

We all have a cycle of behavior. It starts with our thoughts; thoughts create feelings; feelings create rituals that we act out. The behaviors we act out, for good or for bad, create more feelings and the cycle repeats. Our core beliefs will always drive our behavior. Sometimes we are so focused on changing our behavior, rather than changing our "stinkin' thinkin.'"[166] Let's start by looking at how we view God.

THE TRINITY

What's most true about God is relationship. The traditional Christian view of God is through the eyes of the Trinity. **WE ARE MADE IN THE IMAGE OF, OR JUST LIKE, A GOD WHO IS ALREADY IN RELATIONSHIP.** God, through the Trinity, is trying to help us see that we were designed for and can participate in relationship with them and others. Father, Son, and Spirit—

---

[166] Zig Ziglar (2019). *We All Need a Daily Check-Up.* Retrieved from https://www.ziglar.com/quotes/we-all-need-a-daily-check-up-from/.

CHAPTER 10: NEVER TURN AWAY

one God, three persons. They were already interacting in perfect relationship. They created humanity to share in this relationship.

Jesus, when praying to the Father for us, says: "I pray they will all be one, just as you are in me, Father, and I am in you. And may they be in us..."[167] The Trinity is trying to share their relationship with us. They're trying to help us to be like them—relationally secure.

However, our original design has been tainted. Messed up. Our human brokenness prevents us from loving the way They love. The definition of love I use the most is to have someone's best interest in mind. This has always been God's heart toward us. Humanity isn't the problem for God—it's the lies we believe that keep us from *seeing* our true identity and *living in* our true identity.

I used to believe that Jesus had come to save us from God. I now believe that Jesus came to reveal God (Father, Son, and Spirit) to us as savior. Jesus said, "If you've seen me, you've seen the Father," "The Father and I are one." Paul, who wrote most of the New Testament, tells us that Jesus is the visible image of the invisible God and the fullness of the Godhead dwells in Him.[168]

It's sometimes hard to believe that I might be a misguided believer, even how I see Scripture or the "right way" to teach my children.

It's been interesting for me to go back through Scripture and look at it with a different lens. I've changed from seeing God as more conditional. For instance, Jesus' words on the cross: "My God, My God, why have you forsaken me?"[169] The most common interpretation of this Scripture, I heard growing up, is

---

[167] John 17:21 NLT

[168] Colossians 1:15 & 2:9

[169] Mark 15:34

that God can't look on our sin and had to turn away. Actually, this was a familiar Psalm to the Jewish audience that they would have recognized. Jesus is quoting Psalm 22:1, a prophecy of the cross, and farther down in that Chapter it says, "For he did not despise or abhor the affliction of the afflicted; he did not hide his face from me..."[170] This gave me a completely different view. This passage of Scripture causes me to ask more questions, to challenge what I have believed. Where was the Father when Jesus was on the cross? Paul says, "For God was in Christ reconciling the world to himself, no longer counting men's sins against them."[171] God wasn't somewhere else.

I also see other Scriptures supporting this and Jesus' words to his disciples: "All of you will abandon me, but my Father will never abandon me."[172] In John 17, "...that you love them as much as you love me." If God will never abandon Jesus and has a great unchanging love for Him, this is the same truth for us!

In Genesis 1:26-27, God says, "Let us make man in our image...So God created mankind in his own likeness, in the image of God he created them male and female." Then, in verse 28, it says, "God blessed them." It is interesting to look at the word "blessed" in the Hebrew language. We use this word in English sometimes. When someone sneezes, we say "God bless you." But in Hebrew, the word blessed is the word "Barak," which means to kneel and adore. Can you imagine what it must have been like for Adam and Eve to open their eyes to the Creator kneeling and adoring them? It's true that God creates what He loves and He loves what He creates. Many of us think of the term "to

---

[170] Psalm 22:24 NRSVA

[171] 2 Corinthians 5:19

[172] John 16:32

CHAPTER 10: NEVER TURN AWAY

worship God." But one meaning of the word worship has been translated "to ascribe worth." In this sense, God worships us—ascribes worth to us.

Picture the Divine kneeling before you and ascribing to you the worth God put on you when you were created in God's very image.

If you don't understand this, let me give you an example. When my daughter came into this world, in my heart, I knelt and adored her. I didn't physically kneel in the hospital, but my heart did. I said, "I'm all in." I saw this little child, who I had only known for a few seconds, and I would have died for her. Do you think understanding this would help you to think of yourself in a completely different way? It might change how you think of God and see His love and relentless pursuit of you. Never turning away.

If we learn to see this a different way, it becomes a part of our core beliefs and we can operate and function from a sense of security—no longer from a sense of abandonment and shame. This becomes the model for how we respond to our children and becomes the beliefs we live out and potentially pass on to them.

As we understand how God wants to share their life with us (the Trinity), our love for others, especially our children, should be like God's—never turning away.

Jesus didn't come to save us from God. Jesus came to reveal who God is. *"Jesus did not come to change the mind of God about humanity (it did not need changing)! Jesus came to change the mind of humanity about God."*[173]

CONFLICTING CHOICES

Our children may make decisions differently than what we would like, in spite of the values we've tried to pass on to them. Whether

---

[173] Rohr, R. (2008). *Things Hidden: Scripture as Spirituality.* Cincinnati, OH: Franciscan Media. 94.

it's pornography use, cohabitating with their partner, or same-sex orientation, when a child or young adult makes choices different than their family values, this can be tremendously difficult for parents to navigate.

For many years, I have served as a local pastor in a church in Idaho. Often, parents or grandparents would come to me because they were struggling with their children's decisions which were in conflict with their own beliefs or the values they taught them when they were young—especially in the area of sexuality. One of the thoughts people believe is that if we raise our children the "right" way, they won't struggle or stray from the path.

We must remember that Scripture records how God, the original parent, had two kids, Adam and Eve, and they struggled and strayed from the path. If it was about having perfect kids, then for sure God would have gotten it right, don't you think?

A few years ago, I started a group for family members who had kids in the LGBTQ community and were finding it difficult to know how to communicate and relate to their kids. Part of the tension was believing that if parents were loving their kids in the middle of this, they would be condoning their child's behavior. Parents didn't want to compromise. **IF WE STOP LOVING, WE HAVE COMPROMISED.** The way of Christ is to love without agenda. To stop loving violates the law of Christ. Just giving them, as parents, permission "to love your kids in spite of whether their values are identical to yours," was a huge relief for them. One of the key insights expressed was that we can learn to love our kids like God loves us and *this* love isn't based on behavior or decisions. Love wins!

Stay in the game. It's your best chance to stay connected and have influence in your children's lives.

CHAPTER 10: NEVER TURN AWAY

THE STORY OF THE LOST SON[174]

[11]TO ILLUSTRATE THE POINT FURTHER, JESUS TOLD THEM THIS STORY: "A MAN HAD TWO SONS. [12]THE YOUNGER SON TOLD HIS FATHER, 'I WANT MY SHARE OF YOUR ESTATE NOW BEFORE YOU DIE.' SO HIS FATHER AGREED TO DIVIDE HIS WEALTH BETWEEN HIS SONS.

[13]"A FEW DAYS LATER THIS YOUNGER SON PACKED ALL HIS BELONGINGS AND MOVED TO A DISTANT LAND, AND THERE HE WASTED ALL HIS MONEY IN WILD LIVING. [14]ABOUT THE TIME HIS MONEY RAN OUT, A GREAT FAMINE SWEPT OVER THE LAND, AND HE BEGAN TO STARVE. [15]HE PERSUADED A LOCAL FARMER TO HIRE HIM, AND THE MAN SENT HIM INTO HIS FIELDS TO FEED THE PIGS. [16]THE YOUNG MAN BECAME SO HUNGRY THAT EVEN THE PODS HE WAS FEEDING THE PIGS LOOKED GOOD TO HIM. BUT NO ONE GAVE HIM ANYTHING.

[17]"WHEN HE FINALLY CAME TO HIS SENSES, HE SAID TO HIMSELF, 'AT HOME EVEN THE HIRED SERVANTS HAVE FOOD ENOUGH TO SPARE, AND HERE I AM DYING OF HUNGER! [18]I WILL GO HOME TO MY FATHER AND SAY, "FATHER, I HAVE SINNED AGAINST BOTH HEAVEN AND YOU, [19]AND I AM NO LONGER WORTHY OF BEING CALLED YOUR SON. PLEASE TAKE ME ON AS A HIRED SERVANT."'

[20]"SO HE RETURNED HOME TO HIS FATHER. AND WHILE HE WAS STILL A LONG WAY OFF, HIS FATHER SAW HIM COMING. FILLED WITH LOVE AND COMPASSION, HE RAN TO HIS SON, EMBRACED HIM, AND KISSED HIM. [21]HIS SON SAID TO HIM, 'FATHER, I HAVE SINNED

---

[174] Luke 15:11-24 NLT

AGAINST BOTH HEAVEN AND YOU, AND I AM NO LONGER WORTHY OF BEING CALLED YOUR SON.'

[22]"BUT HIS FATHER SAID TO THE SERVANTS, 'QUICK! BRING THE FINEST ROBE IN THE HOUSE AND PUT IT ON HIM. GET A RING FOR HIS FINGER AND SANDALS FOR HIS FEET. [23]AND KILL THE CALF WE HAVE BEEN FATTENING. WE MUST CELEBRATE WITH A FEAST, [24]FOR THIS SON OF MINE WAS DEAD AND HAS NOW RETURNED TO LIFE. HE WAS LOST, BUT NOW HE IS FOUND.' SO THE PARTY BEGAN.

In Luke 15, Jesus tells a story of a son who walked away from his father and didn't want anything to do with him. When the son—who made very poor decisions, that not only hurt others, but hurt himself—finds himself in a pig pen, hungry, and lost, his hope is that at least his father will take him back as a servant. As the son turns back toward the father, he finds not only the father waiting (turned toward him), but running toward him with a full embrace and kiss. As the son started to explain that he was unworthy to be his son, the father immediately stops him and started giving orders to his nearby servant, "Quick, get a robe, get a ring, get new shoes. It's prime rib tonight. Someone call a DJ; we are going to celebrate!"

Some would say that the ring was not just a sign of family wealth but allegiance, inferring that the son could have taken it off at one time, maybe even throwing it at the father as he departed. Yet the father always knew the ring belonged to his son and was able to help him see, "You're not my servant, you're my son—always have been, and always will be." We see the powerful image as we picture the father placing the ring on his son's finger and proclaiming his worth and value, not shaming him for his mistakes.

The son made choices that hurt his father, that his father wouldn't have approved of, and yet, even though the son turned

CHAPTER 10: NEVER TURN AWAY

from the father and even from the truth about himself, the father never turned from his son. The son lost view of his true identity, but the father never did; his response to his son proved this fact for sure! His behavior did not change the truth about his son.

This is the power of love and grace! **OUR VALUE IS NEVER DEPENDENT ON OUR BEHAVIOR.** In my opinion, this is one of the most powerful statements we can say to our kids: "I may be sad about some of your decisions and choices, but I will always love you, and I will never turn away from you."

This is God's heart toward each one of us!

PURITY RINGS

In the 1980s and 90s, there was a focus on the sexual purity of our youth with the purity ring movement. Typically, this was making a promise or religious vow to be sexually abstinent until marriage. I believe the heart behind this movement was for the most part good, wanting our children to make good moral decisions with their sexuality and value themselves.

All of us want our children to make good decisions in every area of their lives. We don't want our children to make choices that will hurt them, even though we know they can also grow through their mistakes.

I had heard of and seen the purity ring or "promise ring" concept, but there was something about it that didn't resonate with me. In thinking about it and talking about what other parents had done in training their children, it raised a lot of questions for me. Is the promise ring based on performance? Does it make kids think, *If I make a mistake, 'lose my purity,' and I've made a promise to my parents and God, and now I've broken it, what happens?* They may also think, *Maybe I'm not going to tell my mom and dad,* which creates more shame and secrets. Our parents and certainly God should be the safest people to come to with our mistakes. Does this possibly raise an issue with shame and guilt that could be the seeds of lifelong baggage young people will carry into their adult lives? Will they think they are damaged goods—that they are a second class Christian? Will our kids think, *I am going to live the rest of my life not in God's perfect will because my sexual sin messed it up!*

Do we just want to teach our kids not to have sexual intercourse until marriage, or is there a bigger message in all this? Isn't it about valuing themselves and others? Are we actually talking to our kids about all areas of what sexual intimacy is—all sexual behavior with others outside of marriage, not just intercourse? As a parent, am I sharing the bigger message of sexuality being best expressed in a committed covenant relationship of marriage? Valuing their own sexuality as a single person? Am I missing teaching them about the picture of respect for others?

Perhaps there's a better way.

Our purity isn't something we just do before marriage. It's a way of life, married or single.

What messages do we want to send to our kids? I believe in a holistic way of thinking about it. Let all of our words, actions, and even rituals come from an approach of acceptance, intrinsic and unchanging worth, and not shame based. I had already felt like I was on plan B in life, because it was such the unpardonable sin, the worst kind of mistake I could make. This wasn't the message I wanted to send to my kids.

Just like I had learned about my heavenly Father, I wanted my kids to know that I would never leave them and their worth does not change regardless of their successes or failures.

This whole chapter is so critical for me. As a parent, more than anything else, I wanted to find a way to express to my

CHAPTER 10: NEVER TURN AWAY

daughter and two sons my heart to never turn away from them regardless of their behavior. The shame and fear that haunted me as a young boy wasn't anything I wanted to pass on to them.

THE VALUE RING

As a father, it's an incredible moment when you walk your daughter down the aisle. Last summer my little curly-haired girl, the one I dropped off at preschool (seems like just a few years ago), got married. As a pastor, I've performed a lot of weddings, so I wanted to sit this one out as just "the dad," but the bride wanted me to perform the ceremony. And you know, "What the bride says goes."

I walked my daughter down the aisle through a chapel in the woods with music playing "You've got me touching heaven," and I was overwhelmed. I started saying to the audience, "This is such a great day. This is such a great day!" This is true, to the amazement of my family, I really did this.

My wife and I agreed it was the best day of our lives. People said, "What do you mean, wasn't your own wedding, births of your children...?" For sure, those are all up at the top of the list, but this day was about all the years that led up to it. Our whole family joining together and throwing a big party—first wedding, first in-law, and two proud younger brothers who took my place at the front, while I stood with the bride. They said,"Who gives this woman...?" I said, "Her mother and brothers and I." These three little kids, who played and fought, shared their first puppy, and grew up to be best friends, now were so excited to share this day!

It was the best day of our lives because we had our own wedding 29 years earlier and this day represented some very beautiful and also some very hard days we had shared together—a whole lot of growing and building our marriage and our family.

As I reflect back, many years earlier, I remember taking that beautiful bride out for her sixteenth birthday. I wanted to find a special way to let her know what I thought about her and, even more, what the Divine thought of her.

When our daughter was turning 16, I said to my wife Traci, "I'd like to take Whitney out on a special date." So, I took her out for her sixteenth birthday, and I said, "Whitney, I want to buy you a ring." We went to get her a manicure and then to a jewelry store to look for a ring for her. We started with the biggest ring we saw, and I said to the sales person, "Can we try on this one?" Whitney tried it on and I asked the person helping us, "How much does this ring cost?" He responded, "Sir, this ring is $10,000." I said to my daughter, "I love it, but it's too bad it doesn't match the color of your eyes. Let's keep looking." We laughed and we kept looking until we found one that fit the budget better, in the hundreds, not the thousands range.

I gave Whitney the ring that night, and I said, "Whitney, this ring is not a promise ring. This is not a ring I'm giving you so that you promise me and your mother that you won't make any mistakes in the area of your sexuality. We want you to navigate this part of your life in a healthy way, but that's not what this ring is about."

Sexuality was not the only area of life where we wanted her to make good decisions. I said, "Whitney, otherwise, you would have to promise me you would never lie, never gossip, never steal, never cheat. You don't have enough fingers and I don't have enough rings for you to make every moral promise." I wasn't interested in having her make some external promise to me for my benefit. I wanted to motivate her to make good decisions out of seeing her internal worth and value.

CHAPTER 10: NEVER TURN AWAY

Then I said to her, "Whitney, this ring is a Value Ring. This is not your promise to us, this is our promise to you. I want you to know that your value in our eyes will never change, regardless of your behavior. Whether you make good decisions in life or you make poor decisions, your worth as our daughter will never change, and we will always love you. Our heart will always be *for* you. If I, as an earthly parent, can love you this much, then how much more does God love us, being our perfect heavenly Father?"

For my wife and I, our intrinsic love for our daughter would never change; our heart of love for her would never turn away.

When our children know their worth and value, it creates a better place from which they make decisions.

That same heart I shared with our daughter that night, now many years ago, continues to be true for all three of our kids. No matter their choices in life, their value never changes to us or to their Creator, and we will never turn away.

CONCLUSION

This book is a work that has developed over many years. Our kids are now young adults, but my wife and I will always be their parents. We have made an effort to keep growing over the decades and continue to grow as individuals and parents. We are clear that we didn't do everything right in parenting, but we have learned to grieve our regrets and continue to pass on new ways of thinking.

My wife and I grew up in an era of thinking that we had to figure everything out. We had to do it all the right way. We needed to try to have all the right answers. But now, we have learned to be question-askers more than statement-makers, being willing to wrestle with the truth and always ask ourselves, "What is 'the better way' that Christ modeled?" Our family has a practice of sitting around a table or in the family room asking questions and discussing beliefs, without having to all agree and end up with the same answer. There is a freedom and safety in not having all the answers and continuing to discover life together.

Since 2013, my wife and I have been closely connected to the organization of Pure Desire Ministries. Even though I had found sobriety in the area of sexual addiction many years prior, there were pieces of my shame that still needed healing. Pure Desire gave me the framework to have the courage to share my story openly, to let go of shame, and to invite others into this same process.

Currently, I lead groups for men and clergy, serve as a board member for Pure Desire, and work as the Advancement Specialist, traveling and speaking with my wife. We are honored to represent and raise funds for this organization, to continue the mission of bringing hope, healing, and education to those who are sexually broken.

We have felt an invitation to participate with God in this global issue, with an urgency to help future generations. Knowing we do this by helping ourselves—becoming healthy adults—so we can be the so-called "tribal elders," sharing our story, paving the way for those who are brave enough to follow.

NEXT STEPS

We hope we've given you a lot to think about. Don't just take our word for it. Begin to think and ask your own questions. Observe what is and isn't working around you, and don't be afraid to let go of old paradigms that simply don't work for you anymore.

In the appendix, we have put together a list of many resources to continue the process of learning. Listen to a lot of voices, not just from your own "tribe"—people who think just like you. Christ is the example to follow, and Christ was always about love first. You can trust the Spirit of God to guide you into His Truth.

We participate in the monthly financial support of this cause, helping parents, couples, and individuals learn to change and grow, leaving a legacy of healthy behaviors for their kids. Would you consider joining us? **To give, visit puredesire.org/give.**

My wife and I are also available to share with you in your church, school, or organization.

If you want to contact us or have any questions or thoughts, here is my cell phone number. Rodney Wright: 208-691-3872 or email us at rodney@puredesire.org or traciw@puredesire.org.

APPENDIX

EMOTIONS/EMOJI CHART

HAPPY   PEACEFUL   CONFIDENT   LOVING   AMUSED

SAD   LONELY   BORED   GUILTY   IGNORED

ANGRY   HURT   HATEFUL   FRUSTRATED   CRITICAL

SCARED   WORRIED   EMBARRASSED   REJECTED   INSECURE

SURPRISED   CONFUSED   EXCITED   DISMAYED   AMAZED

DISGUSTED   DISAPPOINTED   HESITANT   JUDGMENTAL   AWFUL

ROAD TO THE WOUND[175]

INSTRUCTIONS: REMEMBER A SITUATION IN WHICH YOU UNDERREACTED OR OVERREACTED, THE MORE RECENT THE BETTER.

Event That Caused Your Reaction: What happened? What triggered you?

Emotional Under/Overreaction: How did you feel (name the feeling)? How strong was the emotion, with 10 as the strongest? Name the "button" that got pushed (a button is a vulnerability or sore spot).

Reaction: What did you do (Defensive Reaction)?

Your feelings/actions are justified because you believed...what? **What were you telling yourself?**

Who/what else have you reacted this way to? When?

What could you have **done differently**?

True Belief: What does the Bible say about this subject?

---

[175] Dye, M. (2012). *The Genesis Process: For Change Groups, Book 1 and 2, Individual Workbook* (4th ed.). Auburn, CA: Michael Dye. 347.

APPENDIX

RECOMMENDED RESOURCES

WITH KIDS

Learning About Sex Book Series. Concordia Publishing House: https://www.cph.org/c-2910-learning-about-sex.aspx.

PRESCHOOL

Saltz, G. (2005). *Amazing You! Getting Smart About Your Private Parts.* New York, NY: Penguin Group.

Jenson, K. & Poyner, G. (2016). *Good Pictures Bad Pictures: Pornproofing Today's Young Kids.* Richland, WA: Glen Cove Press.

Harris, R. (2008). *It's Not the Stork!: A Book About Girls, Boys, Babies, Bodies, Families and Friends.* Somerville, MA: Candlewick Press.

National Society for the Prevention of Cruelty to Children (2019). Let's Talk Pants: https://www.nspcc.org.uk/preventing-abuse/keeping-children-safe/underwear-rule/

GRADE SCHOOL

Jenson, K. & Poyner, G. (2016). *Good Pictures Bad Pictures: Pornproofing Today's Young Kids.* Richland, WA: Glen Cove Press.

Brown, L. & Brown, M. (1997). *What's the Big Secret? Talking about Sex with Girls and Boys.* New York, NY: Little, Brown Books for Young Readers.

PREADOLESCENT

GIRLS

Natterson, C. (2012). *The Care & Keeping of You 2: The Body Book for Older Girls.* Middleton, WI: American Girl Publishing.

BOYS

Natterson, C. (2017). *Guy Stuff: The Body Book for Boys.* Middleton, WI: American Girl Publishing.

Dunham, K. (2019). *The Boys Body Book: Everything You Need to Know for a Healthy, Happy YOU!* (5th ed.). Kennebunkport, ME: Cider Mill Press Book Publishers.

TEENS

Fortify: www.joinfortify.com.

FOR ADULTS

Culture Reframed. Building Resilience & Resistance To Hypersexualized Media & Porn: culturereframed.org.

Penner, C. & Penner, J. (1992). *Sex Facts for the Family.* Nashville, TN: W Publishing Group.

Roberts, B. & Kolb, H. (2018). *Digital Natives: Raising An Online Generation.* Gresham, OR: Pure Desire Ministries International.

NetSmartz Workshop and Disney have teamed up to offer a self-paced, online training program to help you teach Internet safety and prepare kids to be better digital citizens: https://www.netsmartz.org/Training.

Internet Matters. Helping parents keep their children safe online: www.internetmatters.org.

CovenantEyes Screen Accountability: covenanteyes.com.

Focus on the Family: focusonthefamily.com.

APPENDIX

Texas Christian University (2019). Trust-based relational intervention (TBRI®). TBRI® 101: A Self-Guided Course in Trust-Based Relationships: https://child.tcu.edu/tbri101/#sthash.XtwqGE9a.dpbs.

LGBTQ

Harper, B. & Harper, D. (2016). *Space at the Table: Conversations between an Evangelical Theologian and His Gay Son.* Portland, OR: Zeal Books.

Marin, A. (2009). *Love is an Orientation: Elevating the Conversation with the Gay Community.* Downers Grove, IL: InterVarsity Press.

SUICIDE PREVENTION

National Suicide Prevention Lifeline: https://suicidepreventionlifeline.org/.

PERSONAL HEALTH

Cloud, H. & Townsend, J. (1992). *Boundaries: When to say yes, how to say no to take control of your life.* Grand Rapids, MI: Zondervan.

Cloud, H. & Townsend, J. (1995). *Safe People: How to Find Relationships That Are Good for You and Avoid Those That Aren't.* Grand Rapids, MI: Zondervan.

Cloud, H. (2003). *Changes That Heal: How to Understand Your Past to Ensure a Healthier Future.* Grand Rapids, MI: Zondervan.

Pure Desire Ministries International: puredesire.org.

GROUP PROCESSING

Dye, M. (2012). *The Genesis Process: For Change Groups, Book 1 and 2, Individual Workbook* (4th ed.). Auburn, CA: Michael Dye.

Kolb, H., Jameson, A., Philipsen, A., Flanagan, D., Roberts, D., Moreno, P., & Chinchin, S. (2019). *Unraveled: Managing Love, Sex, and Relationships.* Troutdale, OR: Pure Desire Ministries International.

Roberts, T. (2014). *Seven Pillars of Freedom Workbook.* Gresham, OR: Pure Desire Ministries International.

Roberts, D. (2016). *Betrayal & Beyond Workbook: Fashioning A Courageous Heart.* Gresham, OR: Pure Desire Ministries International.

Wiles, J. (Producer), Wiles, T. (Producer), Melin, J. (Producer) & Wiles, J. (Director). (2013). *Conquer Series: The Battle Plan for Purity* [DVD]. United States: KingdomWorks Studios.

www.ingramcontent.com/pod-product-compliance
Lightning Source LLC
Chambersburg PA
CBHW032223080426
42735CB00008B/686